Ivy Global

SSAT
Upper Level Tests

EDITION 3.0

IVY GLOBAL, NEW YORK

SSAT Upper Level Tests, Edition 3.0

This publication was written and edited by the team at Ivy Global.

Editor-in-Chief: Laurel Perkins

Layout Editor: Sacha Azor

Producers: Lloyd Min and Junho Suh

Contributors: Sarah Boivin, Grace Bueler, Alexandra Candib, Isabel Carlin, Alex Emond, Corwin Henville, Lei Huang, Mark Mendola, Sarah Pike, Yolanda Song, and Isabel Villeneuve

About Ivy Global

Ivy Global is a pioneering education company that provides a wide range of educational services.

E-mail: info@ivyglobal.com

Website: http://www.ivyglobal.com

Contents

Introduction
Chapter 1

Section 1
How to Use this Book

Welcome, students and parents! This book is intended for students preparing for the Verbal, Reading, Writing, and Math sections of the Upper Level Secondary School Admission Test (SSAT). For students applying to many top private and independent schools in North America, the SSAT is a crucial and sometimes daunting step in the admissions process. By leading you step-by-step through the fundamental content and most effective strategies for the SSAT, Ivy Global will help you build your confidence and maximize your score on this important exam.

This book is right for you if:

- you are applying to a private or independent school that requires the SSAT for admission
- you will be in Grades 8-11 (Upper Level) when you write the SSAT
- you would like to practice for the SSAT exam using full-length practice tests under simulated testing conditions
- you are a parent, family member, or tutor looking for new ways to help your Upper Level SSAT student

Ivy Global's *SSAT Upper Level Tests* provides two full-length exams to help students practice for the SSAT under simulated testing conditions. This book includes:

- an up-to-date introduction to the SSAT's administration, format, and scoring practices
- instructions for taking a full-length practice test for the SSAT under simulated testing conditions
- 2 full-length practice tests for the SSAT Upper Level
- detailed scoring instructions for each exam

Work through the exams. After you have finished an exam, take time to assess your strengths and weaknesses. Then, spend some time reviewing the concepts you found challenging before you test yourself again.

To get started, continue reading for an overview of the SSAT and some general test-taking advice. Good luck in this exciting new step for your education!

Section 2
About the SSAT

The **SSAT (Secondary School Admission Test)** is a standardized test administered to students in grades 3-11 to help determine placement into certain private and independent schools. Many secondary schools worldwide use the SSAT as an integral part of their admissions process. The SSAT is owned, published, and developed by the Secondary School Admission Test Board. All tests are printed in English.

You will register for one of three SSAT tests, depending on your grade level:
- The **Elementary Level** exam is for students currently in grades 3-4.
- The **Middle Level** exam (formerly Lower Level) is for students currently in grades 5-7.
- The **Upper Level** exam is for students currently in grades 8-11.

All levels have the same basic format but vary in difficulty and length. The Elementary Level is shorter than the Middle and Upper Levels.

When is the Test Administered?

The SSAT is administered at national test centers on "**Standard**" dates eight times during the academic year. In some locations, regional private schools and organizations also have the option of administering the test independently on non-standard dates. These independent dates are called "**Flex**" test dates, and they are listed by region on the SSAT website at www.ssat.org. It does not matter whether you take the exam on a Standard or Flex test date if both are offered in your location.

How Many Times Can I Take the Test?

In most locations, a student can register for a Standard test as often as desired, up to eight times per academic year. However, a student can only register for a Flex test once per academic year. For students applying to schools in Ontario, the Ontario Testing Consortium allows students to register for only one SSAT test per academic year. Any subsequent attempts to take the exam will be considered invalid and will not be reported to schools.

How Do I Register?

The easiest and fastest way to register is to complete the **online application**. Visit www.ssat.org to register for an exam in your location. The other alternative is to mail or fax a completed form to SSAT by the regular registration deadline.

Make sure to print off and keep the **Admission Ticket** that is obtainable only after SSAT has received and processed your registration and payment. This ticket both serves as a confirmation for your test registration, and includes important details of your pending test: date, location of scheduled test, specific instructions regarding taking the SSAT, and your list of schools and consultants chosen to receive your SSAT scores.

What is the Format of the SSAT?

The SSAT consists of three main sections (**Verbal**, **Math**, and **Reading**), plus a **Writing Sample** that either takes the form of a creative writing assignment or an essay. The format of the test differs based on the level of the exam:

Elementary Level			
Section	Questions	Length	Topics Covered
Math	30 questions	30 min	Arithmetic, geometry, word problems
Verbal	30 questions	20 min	Vocabulary: synonyms and analogies
15-minute break			
Reading	28 questions	30 min	Short passages: fiction, non-fiction, poetry
Writing	1 prompt	15 min	Creative writing assignment (not scored)
Total testing time: 1 hour, 50 minutes			

Middle and Upper Levels			
Section	Questions	Length	Topics Covered
Writing	One prompt	25 min	Creative writing assignment or essay (not scored)
5-minute break			
Math I	25 questions	30 min	Arithmetic, algebra, geometry, word problems
Reading	40 questions	40 min	Short passages: fiction, non-fiction, poetry
10-minute break			
Verbal	60 questions	30 min	Vocabulary: synonyms and analogies
Math II	25 questions	30 min	Arithmetic, algebra, geometry, word problems
Experimental Section	16 questions	15 min	Varies: this section is testing out questions for upcoming years and is not scored
Total testing time: 3 hours, 5 minutes			

Except for the Writing Sample, all questions are **multiple choice** (A) to (E). You are not allowed to use calculators, rulers, dictionaries, or other aids during the exam.

How is the SSAT Scored?

All of the multiple-choice questions on the SSAT are equal in value, and your **raw score** for these sections is calculated as follows:

- One mark is given for every question answered correctly.
- $\frac{1}{4}$ mark is deducted for every question answered incorrectly.
- No marks are awarded or deducted for questions left blank.

Therefore, your raw score is the number of questions you answer correctly subtracted by one quarter point for each question you answer incorrectly.

Your raw score is then converted into a **scaled score** for each section (Verbal, Math, and Reading) that represents how well you did in comparison to the other students taking the same exam:

- Elementary Level scaled score: 300-600 for each section, 900-1800 total
- Middle Level scaled score: 440-710 for each section, 1320-2130 total
- Upper Level scaled score: 500-800 for each section, 1500-2400 total

The **Writing Sample** is not scored, but is sent to the schools you are applying to as a sample of your writing skills. Admissions officers may use your essay or story to evaluate your writing ability when they are making admissions decisions.

The **Experimental Section** on the Middle and Upper Levels is the SSAT's method of testing out new questions for upcoming years. The section is not scored, but students should try to complete it to the best of their ability. The section may include any mixture of Verbal, Reading, or Math questions.

Scores are released to families and to the schools that families have designated as recipients within two weeks after the test date. Schools receive a printed report by mail and an electronic copy online. Families receive an electronic copy and can request a printed report for an extra fee. You may designate certain schools as recipients during registration, or at any time before or after testing through your online account at www.ssat.org.

What are the SSAT Percentiles?

The SSAT score report also provides **SSAT percentile** rankings for each category, comparing your performance to that of other students in the same grade who have taken the test in the past three years. If you score in the 60th percentile, this means you scored higher than 60% of other students in your grade taking the exam.

These percentile rankings provide a more accurate way of evaluating student performance at each grade level. However, the SSAT percentiles only compare your score to those of other students who have taken the SSAT, and these tend to be very high-achieving students. Students should not be discouraged if their percentile rankings appear low.

Because the Elementary Level exam was first administered in 2012, percentile data for this test has not yet been released.

	Median Scores (SSAT 50th Percentile)			
	Grade	Reading	Verbal	Quantitative
	5	585	590	587
Middle Level	6	603	610	611
	7	628	635	635
	8	647	660	676
	9	653	667	699
Upper Level	10	659	670	705
	11	647	656	704

The SSAT also publishes an Estimated National Percentile Ranking for test takers in grades 5-9, which provides an estimated comparison of student performance against the entire national student population, not just the set of students taking the SSAT. The test also provides a projected SAT score for test-takers in grades 7-10.

How Do Schools Use the SSAT?

Schools use the SSAT as one way to assess potential applicants, but it is by no means the only tool that they are using. Schools also pay very close attention to the rest of the student's application—academic record, teacher recommendations, extracurricular activities, writing samples, and interviews—in order to determine which students might be the best fit for their program. The personal components of a student's application give schools a lot more information about the student's personality and potential contributions to the school's overall community. Different schools place a different amount of importance on SSAT and other test scores within this process, and admissions offices are good places to find how much your schools of interest will weight the SSAT.

Test-Taking Strategies
Chapter 2

Section 1
Approaching the SSAT

Before you review the content covered on the SSAT, you need to focus on *how* you take the SSAT. If you approach the SSAT *thoughtfully* and *strategically*, you will avoid common traps and tricks planted in the SSAT by the test makers. Think of the SSAT as a timed maze—you need to make every turn cleverly and quickly so that you avoid getting stuck at a dead end with no time to spare.

In this section, you will learn about the SSAT's format and structure; this awareness will help you avoid any surprises or shocks on test day. A very predictable exam, the SSAT will seem less challenging once you understand what it looks like and how it works. By learning strategies and techniques for best test-taking practice, you will discover how to work as quickly and intelligently as possible. Once you know what to expect, you can refine your knowledge of the content tested on the SSAT, such as the verbal and math skills that are based on your grade level in school.

This section on SSAT strategies will answer your major questions:

- How does the SSAT differ from a test you take in school?
- What preparation strategies can you learn before you take the SSAT?
- What strategies can you learn to use during the SSAT?
- How can you manage stress before and during the SSAT?

In the process of answering your big questions, this section will also highlight key facts about smart test-taking:

- Your answer choice matters—your process does not. Grid your answer choices correctly and carefully to earn points. You have a set amount of time per section, so spend it wisely.
- The SSAT's format and directions do not change, so learn them now.
- All questions have the same value.
- Each level of the SSAT corresponds to a range of grades, and score expectations differ based on your grade level.
- Identify your areas of strength and weakness, and review any content that feels unfamiliar.

- Apply universal strategies—prediction-making, Process of Elimination, back-solving, and educated guessing—to the multiple-choice sections.
- Stay calm and be confident in your abilities as you prepare for and take the SSAT.

How Does the SSAT Differ from a Test You Take in School?
Part 1

The SSAT differs from assessments you take in school in four major ways:

1. It is not concerned with the process behind your answers. Your answer is either right or wrong; there is no partial credit.
2. You have a set amount of time per section (and for the exam as a whole).
3. It is divided into three levels that correspond to three grade ranges of students.
4. It is extremely predictable given that its format, structure, and directions never vary.

No Partial Credit

At this point in your school career, you have probably heard your teacher remark, "Be sure to show your work on the test!" You are most likely familiar with almost every teacher's policy of "No work, no credit." However, the SSAT completely ignores this guideline. The machine that grades your exam does not care that you penciled brilliant logic in the margins of the test booklet—the machine only looks at your gridded answer choice. Your answer choice is either right or wrong; **there is no partial credit**.

Set Amount of Time

You have a **set amount of time per section**, so spend it wisely. The SSAT test proctors will never award you extra time after a test section has ended because you spent half of one section struggling valiantly on a single problem. Instead, you must learn to work within each section's time constraints.

You also must view the questions as equal because **each question is worth one point**. Even though some questions are more challenging than others, they all carry the same weight. Rather than dwell on a problem, you should skip it, work through the rest of the section, and come back to it if you have time.

Three Levels

There are three levels of the SSAT—Elementary, Middle, and Upper—each of which is administered to a specific range of students. The Elementary Level is given to students in grades 3 and 4; the Middle Level is given to students in grades 5, 6, and 7; and the Upper Level is given to students in grades 8, 9, 10, and 11. While you might be used to taking tests in school that are completely tailored to your grade, the SSAT is different: each test level covers content from a specific range of grade levels.

Score expectations differ based on your grade level. You are not expected to answer as many questions correctly on a Middle Level exam if you are only in fifth grade. Conversely, if you are in seventh grade, you are expected to answer the most questions correctly on the Middle Level exam because you are one of the oldest students taking that exam.

Standard Format

The SSAT is, by definition, a **standardized test**, which means that its format and directions are standard and predictable. While your teachers might change formats and directions for every assessment they administer, you can expect to see the same format and directions on every SSAT.

What Preparation Strategies Can You Learn Before You Take the SSAT?
Part 2

Now that you are familiar with how the SSAT differs from the tests you take in school, you are ready to learn some test tips. You can prepare for the SSAT by following these three steps:

- Learn the format and directions of the test.
- Identify your areas of strength and weakness.
- Create a study schedule to review and practice test content.

Learn the Format and Directions

The structure of the SSAT is entirely predictable, so learn this now. Rather than wasting precious time reading the directions and understanding the format on test day, take the time now to familiarize yourself with the test's format and directions.

Refer to the tables on page 6 and 7 for an overview of the SSAT's format. Specific directions for the Verbal, Reading, and Writing sections can be found in Ivy Global's *SSAT English*. Specific directions for the math section can be found in Ivy Global's *SSAT Math*.

Identify Your Strengths and Weaknesses

To determine your areas of strength and weakness and identify which concepts you need to review, take a full-length, accurate practice exam to serve as a diagnostic test. Two full-length practice exams can be found in this book for the Upper Level.

Make sure you simulate test day conditions by timing yourself. Then, check your answers against the correct answers. Write down how many questions you missed in each section, and note the topics or types of questions you found most challenging (e.g. analogies, fiction passages, geometry, or data analysis). What was hard about the test? What did you feel good about? Did you leave a lot of questions blank because of timing issues, or did you leave questions blank because you did not know how to solve them? Reflecting on these questions, in addition to looking at your score breakdown, will help you determine your strengths, weaknesses, and areas for improvement.

Create a Study Schedule

After determining your areas of strength and weakness, create a study plan and schedule for your SSAT preparation to review content. Work backward from your test date until you arrive at your starting point for studying. The number of weeks you have until your exam will determine how much time you can (and should) devote to your preparation. Remember, practice is the most important thing!

To begin, try using this sample study plan as a model for your own personalized study schedule.

Sample Study Plan

My test date is: _____.

I have _____ weeks to study. I will make an effort to study _____ minutes/hours every day/week, and I will set aside extra time on _____ to take timed sections.

I plan to take _____ full-length tests between now and my test date. I will study for _____ weeks and then take a practice test. My goal for this test is to improve my score in the following specific areas:

_____

_____

_____

_____

_____

_____

_____

_____

_____

If I do not make this goal, then I will spend more time studying.

Study Schedule				
Date	Plan of Study	Time Allotted	Time Spent	Goal Reached?
1/1	Learn 5 words and review perimeter of polygons	1 hour	44 minutes	Yes, I know 5 new words and can calculate perimeter!
1/3	Learn 5 words and review area of triangles	1 hour	1 hour	I know 5 new words, but I'm still confused about the area of triangles. I'll review this again next time and ask a teacher, tutor, or parent for help.

What Strategies Can You Learn to Use During the Test?

Part 3

Once you have grown accustomed to the SSAT through practice, you are ready to learn strategies to use during the SSAT. The following points will prepare you to take the test as cleverly and efficiently as possible:

- Grid your answer choices correctly and carefully.
- Pace yourself to manage your time effectively.
- Learn a strategic approach for multiple-choice questions.

Gridding Answer Choices

For the Middle and Upper Level exams, you must enter your answers on a separate answer sheet. In school you probably take tests that, for the most part, do not ask you to transfer your answers to a separate sheet. However, the SSAT streamlines the grading process by only reviewing your answer sheet. You must grid in your multiple-choice answers onto this sheet using an HB pencil to fill in the circle that corresponds to your answer. This sheet is scanned and scored by a highly sensitive computer. You will also write your Writing Sample on separate lined pages of this answer sheet.

Since you have to take an additional step to record your answers, it is important that you avoid making gridding mistakes. Sadly, many students get confused and mismark their answer sheets. Remember, even if you arrive at the right answer, it is only correct and counted in your favor if you grid correctly on your answer sheet.

To grid correctly and carefully to maximize your points, consider the following tips:

Keep your answer sheet neat. Since your answer sheet is graded by a machine, your score is calculated based on what your marks look like. The machine cannot know what you really meant if you picked the wrong bubble. Stray marks can harm your score, especially if you darken the correct answer but accidentally make a mark that confuses the machine! Avoid this and other errors by consulting the following image, which shows the difference between answers that are properly shaded and those that are not.

1. Ⓐ Ⓑ Ⓒ Ⓓ̶ Ⓔ   X   Answer 1 is wrong because no answer is selected and there are stray marks.

2. Ⓐ Ⓑ Ⓒ Ⓓ Ⓔ   X   Answer 2 is neither right nor wrong because it was left blank.

3. Ⓐ Ⓑ Ⓒ̶Ⓓ̶ Ⓔ   X   Answer 3 is wrong because two answers have been selected.

4. Ⓐ Ⓑ Ⓒ ● Ⓔ   X   Answer 4 is wrong because two answers have been selected.

5. Ⓐ Ⓑ Ⓒ Ⓓ ☒   X   Answer 5 is wrong because choice (E) has not been darkened properly and there are stray marks.

6. ● Ⓑ Ⓒ Ⓓ Ⓔ   ✓   Answer 6 is right because choice (A) has been darkened properly.

Train yourself to **circle your answer choice in your test booklet**. If you have time to go back and check your answers, you can easily check your circled answers against your gridded ones.

You should also **create a system for marking questions that you skipped** or that you found confusing (see the next section for more information about skipping around). Try circling those question numbers only in your test booklet so that you can find them if you want to solve them later or check your work. Be aware of these questions when gridding answers on your answer sheet.

Finally, **grid your answers in batches of four, five, or six answer choices.** That way, you do not have to go back and forth between your test booklet and your answer sheet every minute. If you choose to use this strategy, keep an eye on the clock—you do not want to get to the end of the section and find you have not gridded any answers. Depending on how much time you have left to check your work (if you happen to finish early), you can either review every problem or spot-check a series of questions on your answer sheet against your test booklet.

Time Management (Pacing)

Manage your time effectively to boost your score. Just as effective gridding contributes to time management, other strategies enable you to work efficiently and maximize the number of problems you answer. Specifically, skipping questions is particularly important because you need to learn to keep moving on the exam rather than wasting too much time on any single question.

You can skip questions within each section of the SSAT; the freedom to skip questions is helpful since each question is worth only one point. If you are stuck on a problem, you should move on after a minute or two and try to answer another problem. It makes more sense to answer as many questions as possible (and get as many points as possible) rather than spending all your time on one question. If you come across a question you want to skip, mark it in your question booklet (by circling it, underlining it, etc.) and move to the next question; just be sure to skip the corresponding number on your answer sheet if you choose to skip questions. Remember not to make any stray marks on your answer sheet.

There is a benefit to skipping questions. By moving quickly through each question of the section, you will ensure that: 1) you see every question in the section; 2) you gain points on questions that are easy for you; 3) you return to more challenging problems and hopefully answer as many as you can with your remaining time. It is also important to note that you might not be able to answer several questions in each section if you are on the younger end of the testing group for your particular test level. In that case, you should skip those questions unless you can eliminate one or more answer choices. Also, think about the value of skipping in terms of the guessing penalty. If you cannot make a clever guess on a hard problem, then you should skip it and move on because choosing a random answer will most likely cause you to lose one quarter of a point.

Follow this step-by-step process to decide when to skip questions:

1. Look through the section and answer the questions that are easy for you first. Circle any questions that you are not sure about or seem harder.
2. After answering all the easier questions, go back to the questions you have circled and spend some time working on ones that you think you might be able to solve.
3. Skip any questions that you have no idea how to solve.

Continue reading for more detailed information about the guessing penalty and guessing strategies.

Strategies for Multiple-Choice Questions

Apply universal strategies—prediction-making, Process of Elimination, back-solving, and educated guessing—to the multiple-choice sections. To illustrate the value of these strategies, read through the following example of a synonym question from the Verbal Section:

Example
HAPPY:
(A) delighted
(B) unhappy
(C) crazy
(D) nice
(E) depressed

Answer: (A). "Delighted" is the correct answer because it is the word that most nearly means "happy."

Regardless of whether the answer choices are easy, difficult, or somewhere in between, you can use certain tricks and tips to your advantage. To approach SSAT questions effectively, you need to step into the test makers' minds and learn to use their traps against them.

Make predictions. When you see a question, try to come up with an answer on your own before looking at the answer choices. You can literally cover the answer choices with your hand so that you must rely on your own intelligence to predict an answer instead of being swayed by answer choices that you see. If you look at the answer choices first, you might be tempted to circle a choice without thinking about the other options and what the question is asking you. Instead, make a prediction so that you understand the question fully and get a clear sense of what to look for in the answers. In the synonym example above, you could predict that a possible synonym for "happy" would be something like "glad."

Use the **Process of Elimination**. For each multiple-choice question, the answer is always right in front of you. To narrow down your answer choices, actively identify obviously incorrect answers and eliminate them. Even if you can eliminate just one answer, you will set yourself up for better odds if you decide to guess. For the synonym example above, test your prediction of "glad" against the answer choices and immediately eliminate "unhappy" and "depressed" since they are nearly opposite in meaning. You can also probably eliminate "crazy" and "nice" since those words do not match your prediction as well as "delighted," which is the correct answer.

Try back-solving. This strategy is most useful on the math sections, especially when you are given a complicated, multi-step word problem. Instead of writing an equation, try plugging in the answer choices to the word problem. Take a look at the following question:

Example

Catherine has a basket of candy. On Monday, she eats ½ of all the candy. On Tuesday, she eats 2 pieces. On Wednesday, she eats twice the amount of candy that she consumed on Tuesday. If she only has 4 pieces left on Thursday, how many pieces did she initially have?

(A) 12
(B) 14
(C) 16
(D) 20
(E) 22

To use back-solving, start with answer choice (C) and plug it into the word problem. If (C) is the correct answer, you are done. If not, you will then know whether you should test (B) or (D). On the SSAT, numerical answer options are always listed in either ascending or descending order, from least to greatest or from greatest to least, meaning that even if (C) is incorrect, you will then be able to identify whether your answer should be larger or smaller than (C); you can then test (B) or (D) accordingly.

When we start with 16 pieces of candy, we subtract 8 on Monday, then 4 more for Tuesday, and then 2 more for Wednesday. By Thursday, Catherine only has two pieces of candy left, which is less than the amount we wanted. Therefore, we know our answer has to be bigger, so we eliminate choices (A), (B), and (C) and try (D), which works.

(*Fun Fact:* If you think about it, you will only ever have to plug in three answer choices at most to determine the right answer.)

Use educated guessing. Before taking any test, it is important to understand the test's grading rules for correct answers, incorrect answers, and blank answers. The SSAT has a **wrong-answer penalty** for all three levels of the test, which means:

- You lose one quarter of a point from your total score for each question you answer incorrectly.
- You receive one point for every question you answer correctly.
- If you leave a question blank, you do not lose points—but you do not gain points either (so your score will not reach the highest possible range).

The SSAT's penalty is often referred to as a guessing penalty since its purpose is to discourage random guessing. If you did not lose points for guessing, then you could possibly pick the same answer choice for an entire section and get twenty percent of the questions—or more—correct. Thus, the guessing penalty is important because it makes sure your score reflects your abilities rather than your luck when guessing.

Guessing cleverly can certainly improve your score. If you can rule out one or two choices for a tricky question, then you should guess because your chances for guessing correctly are above average. However, if you cannot eliminate any of the answer choices, then guessing is not worth the risk of a quarter-point penalty. In that case, leave the answer blank and move on quickly to gain points on other questions.

Armed with these strategies, you might feel that SSAT is starting to look more manageable because you now have shortcuts that will help you navigate the maze of questions quickly and cleverly.

Take a look at this example to practice using the strategies you just read about.

Example
Doll is to toy as pasta is to
(A) mall
(B) Italy
(C) America
(D) dessert
(E) food

1. Assess the question and recognize what it is testing. In this case, the question tests whether you can complete the analogy.
2. Make a prediction. A doll is a type of toy, so pasta must be a type of something. How about "dinner"?

3. Look for inaccurate answer choices and eliminate them. "Mall" does not make sense. "Italy" and "America" both make pasta, but they are not examples of food or dinner. Dessert is a type of food, but pasta is not a dessert. "Food" is the only possible answer in this case.

4. Make an educated guess, or choose the best answer if you feel confident about it. Since you made a fantastic prediction and used Process of Elimination, you only have one choice left: (E). "Food" is the correct answer—you just earned yourself a point!

How Can You Manage Your Stress?
Part 4

It is natural to be nervous leading up to your exam. However, if that feeling starts to become overwhelming, here are some strategies that you can use. Many of these suggestions are good ideas to use in everyday life, but they become especially important in the final week before your test and on test day itself.

- **Relax and slow down.** To center yourself and ease your nerves, take a big, deep breath. Slowly inhale for a few seconds and then slowly exhale for a few seconds. Shut your eyes and relax. Stretch your arms, roll your neck gently, crack your knuckles—get in the zone of Zen! Continue to breathe deeply and slowly until you can literally feel your body calm down.

- **Picture your goals.** Close your eyes or just pause to reflect on what you want to achieve on test day. Visualize your success; acknowledge your former successes and abilities, and believe in yourself.

- **Break it down.** Instead of trying to study a whole section at once, break up your studying into small and manageable chunks. Outline your study goals before you start. For example, instead of trying to master the entire Reading Section at once, you might want to work on one type of passage at a time.

- **Sleep.** Make sure you get plenty of rest and sleep, especially the two nights leading up to your exam.

- **Fuel up.** Eat healthy, filling meals that fuel your brain. Also, drink lots of water to stay hydrated.

- **Take a break.** Put down the books and go play outside, read, listen to music, exercise, or talk to a trusted friend or family member. A good break can be just as restful as a nap. However, watching television will provide minimal relaxation.

On the night before the exam, study only lightly. Make a list of your three biggest fears and work on them, but don't try to learn anything new. Pick out what you are going to wear to the exam—try wearing layers in case the exam room is hotter or colder than you expect. Organize everything you need to bring, including your Admissions Ticket. Know where the test center is located and how long it will take to get there. Have a nutritious meal and get plenty of sleep!

On the morning of the exam, let your adrenaline kick in naturally. Eat a good breakfast and stay hydrated; your body needs fuel to endure the test. Bring along several pencils and a good eraser. Listen carefully to the test proctor's instructions and let the proctor know if you are left-handed so you can sit in an appropriate desk. Take a deep breath and remember: you are smart and accomplished! Believe in yourself and you will do just fine.

Practice Tests

Chapter 3

Practice Test 1

How to Take this Practice Test

To simulate an accurate testing environment, sit at a desk in a quiet location free of distractions—no TV, computers, phones, music, or noise—and clear your desk of all materials except pencils and erasers. Remember that no calculators, rulers, protractors, dictionaries, or other aids are allowed on the SSAT.

Give yourself the following amounts of time for each section:

Section	Subject	Time Limit
	Writing	25 minutes
5-minute break		
1	Math I	30 minutes
2	Reading	40 minutes
5-minute break		
3	Verbal	30 minutes
4	Math II	30 minutes

Have an adult help you monitor your time, or use a stopwatch and time yourself. Only give yourself the allotted time for each section; put your pencil down when your time is up. Note: timing may be extended for students with diagnosed learning disabilities who apply for testing with accommodations.

Follow the instructions carefully. As you take your test, bubble your answers into the answer sheets provided. Use the test booklet as scratch paper for notes and calculations. Remember that you are not granted time at the end of a section to transfer your answers to the answer sheet, so you must do this as you go along.

When you are finished, check your answers against the answer keys provided. Then, score your exam using the directions at the end.

Be sure each mark completely fills the answer space.
Start with number 1 for each new section of the test. You may find more answer spaces than you need.
If so, please leave them blank.

SECTION 1

1. Ⓐ Ⓑ Ⓒ Ⓓ Ⓔ	6. Ⓐ Ⓑ Ⓒ Ⓓ Ⓔ	11. Ⓐ Ⓑ Ⓒ Ⓓ Ⓔ	16. Ⓐ Ⓑ Ⓒ Ⓓ Ⓔ	21. Ⓐ Ⓑ Ⓒ Ⓓ Ⓔ
2. Ⓐ Ⓑ Ⓒ Ⓓ Ⓔ	7. Ⓐ Ⓑ Ⓒ Ⓓ Ⓔ	12. Ⓐ Ⓑ Ⓒ Ⓓ Ⓔ	17. Ⓐ Ⓑ Ⓒ Ⓓ Ⓔ	22. Ⓐ Ⓑ Ⓒ Ⓓ Ⓔ
3. Ⓐ Ⓑ Ⓒ Ⓓ Ⓔ	8. Ⓐ Ⓑ Ⓒ Ⓓ Ⓔ	13. Ⓐ Ⓑ Ⓒ Ⓓ Ⓔ	18. Ⓐ Ⓑ Ⓒ Ⓓ Ⓔ	23. Ⓐ Ⓑ Ⓒ Ⓓ Ⓔ
4. Ⓐ Ⓑ Ⓒ Ⓓ Ⓔ	9. Ⓐ Ⓑ Ⓒ Ⓓ Ⓔ	14. Ⓐ Ⓑ Ⓒ Ⓓ Ⓔ	19. Ⓐ Ⓑ Ⓒ Ⓓ Ⓔ	24. Ⓐ Ⓑ Ⓒ Ⓓ Ⓔ
5. Ⓐ Ⓑ Ⓒ Ⓓ Ⓔ	10. Ⓐ Ⓑ Ⓒ Ⓓ Ⓔ	15. Ⓐ Ⓑ Ⓒ Ⓓ Ⓔ	20. Ⓐ Ⓑ Ⓒ Ⓓ Ⓔ	25. Ⓐ Ⓑ Ⓒ Ⓓ Ⓔ

SECTION 2

1. Ⓐ Ⓑ Ⓒ Ⓓ Ⓔ	9. Ⓐ Ⓑ Ⓒ Ⓓ Ⓔ	17. Ⓐ Ⓑ Ⓒ Ⓓ Ⓔ	25. Ⓐ Ⓑ Ⓒ Ⓓ Ⓔ	33. Ⓐ Ⓑ Ⓒ Ⓓ Ⓔ
2. Ⓐ Ⓑ Ⓒ Ⓓ Ⓔ	10. Ⓐ Ⓑ Ⓒ Ⓓ Ⓔ	18. Ⓐ Ⓑ Ⓒ Ⓓ Ⓔ	26. Ⓐ Ⓑ Ⓒ Ⓓ Ⓔ	34. Ⓐ Ⓑ Ⓒ Ⓓ Ⓔ
3. Ⓐ Ⓑ Ⓒ Ⓓ Ⓔ	11. Ⓐ Ⓑ Ⓒ Ⓓ Ⓔ	19. Ⓐ Ⓑ Ⓒ Ⓓ Ⓔ	27. Ⓐ Ⓑ Ⓒ Ⓓ Ⓔ	35. Ⓐ Ⓑ Ⓒ Ⓓ Ⓔ
4. Ⓐ Ⓑ Ⓒ Ⓓ Ⓔ	12. Ⓐ Ⓑ Ⓒ Ⓓ Ⓔ	20. Ⓐ Ⓑ Ⓒ Ⓓ Ⓔ	28. Ⓐ Ⓑ Ⓒ Ⓓ Ⓔ	36. Ⓐ Ⓑ Ⓒ Ⓓ Ⓔ
5. Ⓐ Ⓑ Ⓒ Ⓓ Ⓔ	13. Ⓐ Ⓑ Ⓒ Ⓓ Ⓔ	21. Ⓐ Ⓑ Ⓒ Ⓓ Ⓔ	29. Ⓐ Ⓑ Ⓒ Ⓓ Ⓔ	37. Ⓐ Ⓑ Ⓒ Ⓓ Ⓔ
6. Ⓐ Ⓑ Ⓒ Ⓓ Ⓔ	14. Ⓐ Ⓑ Ⓒ Ⓓ Ⓔ	22. Ⓐ Ⓑ Ⓒ Ⓓ Ⓔ	30. Ⓐ Ⓑ Ⓒ Ⓓ Ⓔ	38. Ⓐ Ⓑ Ⓒ Ⓓ Ⓔ
7. Ⓐ Ⓑ Ⓒ Ⓓ Ⓔ	15. Ⓐ Ⓑ Ⓒ Ⓓ Ⓔ	23. Ⓐ Ⓑ Ⓒ Ⓓ Ⓔ	31. Ⓐ Ⓑ Ⓒ Ⓓ Ⓔ	39. Ⓐ Ⓑ Ⓒ Ⓓ Ⓔ
8. Ⓐ Ⓑ Ⓒ Ⓓ Ⓔ	16. Ⓐ Ⓑ Ⓒ Ⓓ Ⓔ	24. Ⓐ Ⓑ Ⓒ Ⓓ Ⓔ	32. Ⓐ Ⓑ Ⓒ Ⓓ Ⓔ	40. Ⓐ Ⓑ Ⓒ Ⓓ Ⓔ

SECTION 3

1. Ⓐ Ⓑ Ⓒ Ⓓ Ⓔ	13. Ⓐ Ⓑ Ⓒ Ⓓ Ⓔ	25. Ⓐ Ⓑ Ⓒ Ⓓ Ⓔ	37. Ⓐ Ⓑ Ⓒ Ⓓ Ⓔ	49. Ⓐ Ⓑ Ⓒ Ⓓ Ⓔ
2. Ⓐ Ⓑ Ⓒ Ⓓ Ⓔ	14. Ⓐ Ⓑ Ⓒ Ⓓ Ⓔ	26. Ⓐ Ⓑ Ⓒ Ⓓ Ⓔ	38. Ⓐ Ⓑ Ⓒ Ⓓ Ⓔ	50. Ⓐ Ⓑ Ⓒ Ⓓ Ⓔ
3. Ⓐ Ⓑ Ⓒ Ⓓ Ⓔ	15. Ⓐ Ⓑ Ⓒ Ⓓ Ⓔ	27. Ⓐ Ⓑ Ⓒ Ⓓ Ⓔ	39. Ⓐ Ⓑ Ⓒ Ⓓ Ⓔ	51. Ⓐ Ⓑ Ⓒ Ⓓ Ⓔ
4. Ⓐ Ⓑ Ⓒ Ⓓ Ⓔ	16. Ⓐ Ⓑ Ⓒ Ⓓ Ⓔ	28. Ⓐ Ⓑ Ⓒ Ⓓ Ⓔ	40. Ⓐ Ⓑ Ⓒ Ⓓ Ⓔ	52. Ⓐ Ⓑ Ⓒ Ⓓ Ⓔ
5. Ⓐ Ⓑ Ⓒ Ⓓ Ⓔ	17. Ⓐ Ⓑ Ⓒ Ⓓ Ⓔ	29. Ⓐ Ⓑ Ⓒ Ⓓ Ⓔ	41. Ⓐ Ⓑ Ⓒ Ⓓ Ⓔ	53. Ⓐ Ⓑ Ⓒ Ⓓ Ⓔ
6. Ⓐ Ⓑ Ⓒ Ⓓ Ⓔ	18. Ⓐ Ⓑ Ⓒ Ⓓ Ⓔ	30. Ⓐ Ⓑ Ⓒ Ⓓ Ⓔ	42. Ⓐ Ⓑ Ⓒ Ⓓ Ⓔ	54. Ⓐ Ⓑ Ⓒ Ⓓ Ⓔ
7. Ⓐ Ⓑ Ⓒ Ⓓ Ⓔ	19. Ⓐ Ⓑ Ⓒ Ⓓ Ⓔ	31. Ⓐ Ⓑ Ⓒ Ⓓ Ⓔ	43. Ⓐ Ⓑ Ⓒ Ⓓ Ⓔ	55. Ⓐ Ⓑ Ⓒ Ⓓ Ⓔ
8. Ⓐ Ⓑ Ⓒ Ⓓ Ⓔ	20. Ⓐ Ⓑ Ⓒ Ⓓ Ⓔ	32. Ⓐ Ⓑ Ⓒ Ⓓ Ⓔ	44. Ⓐ Ⓑ Ⓒ Ⓓ Ⓔ	56. Ⓐ Ⓑ Ⓒ Ⓓ Ⓔ
9. Ⓐ Ⓑ Ⓒ Ⓓ Ⓔ	21. Ⓐ Ⓑ Ⓒ Ⓓ Ⓔ	33. Ⓐ Ⓑ Ⓒ Ⓓ Ⓔ	45. Ⓐ Ⓑ Ⓒ Ⓓ Ⓔ	57. Ⓐ Ⓑ Ⓒ Ⓓ Ⓔ
10. Ⓐ Ⓑ Ⓒ Ⓓ Ⓔ	22. Ⓐ Ⓑ Ⓒ Ⓓ Ⓔ	34. Ⓐ Ⓑ Ⓒ Ⓓ Ⓔ	46. Ⓐ Ⓑ Ⓒ Ⓓ Ⓔ	58. Ⓐ Ⓑ Ⓒ Ⓓ Ⓔ
11. Ⓐ Ⓑ Ⓒ Ⓓ Ⓔ	23. Ⓐ Ⓑ Ⓒ Ⓓ Ⓔ	35. Ⓐ Ⓑ Ⓒ Ⓓ Ⓔ	47. Ⓐ Ⓑ Ⓒ Ⓓ Ⓔ	59. Ⓐ Ⓑ Ⓒ Ⓓ Ⓔ
12. Ⓐ Ⓑ Ⓒ Ⓓ Ⓔ	24. Ⓐ Ⓑ Ⓒ Ⓓ Ⓔ	36. Ⓐ Ⓑ Ⓒ Ⓓ Ⓔ	48. Ⓐ Ⓑ Ⓒ Ⓓ Ⓔ	60. Ⓐ Ⓑ Ⓒ Ⓓ Ⓔ

SECTION 4

1. Ⓐ Ⓑ Ⓒ Ⓓ Ⓔ	6. Ⓐ Ⓑ Ⓒ Ⓓ Ⓔ	11. Ⓐ Ⓑ Ⓒ Ⓓ Ⓔ	16. Ⓐ Ⓑ Ⓒ Ⓓ Ⓔ	21. Ⓐ Ⓑ Ⓒ Ⓓ Ⓔ
2. Ⓐ Ⓑ Ⓒ Ⓓ Ⓔ	7. Ⓐ Ⓑ Ⓒ Ⓓ Ⓔ	12. Ⓐ Ⓑ Ⓒ Ⓓ Ⓔ	17. Ⓐ Ⓑ Ⓒ Ⓓ Ⓔ	22. Ⓐ Ⓑ Ⓒ Ⓓ Ⓔ
3. Ⓐ Ⓑ Ⓒ Ⓓ Ⓔ	8. Ⓐ Ⓑ Ⓒ Ⓓ Ⓔ	13. Ⓐ Ⓑ Ⓒ Ⓓ Ⓔ	18. Ⓐ Ⓑ Ⓒ Ⓓ Ⓔ	23. Ⓐ Ⓑ Ⓒ Ⓓ Ⓔ
4. Ⓐ Ⓑ Ⓒ Ⓓ Ⓔ	9. Ⓐ Ⓑ Ⓒ Ⓓ Ⓔ	14. Ⓐ Ⓑ Ⓒ Ⓓ Ⓔ	19. Ⓐ Ⓑ Ⓒ Ⓓ Ⓔ	24. Ⓐ Ⓑ Ⓒ Ⓓ Ⓔ
5. Ⓐ Ⓑ Ⓒ Ⓓ Ⓔ	10. Ⓐ Ⓑ Ⓒ Ⓓ Ⓔ	15. Ⓐ Ⓑ Ⓒ Ⓓ Ⓔ	20. Ⓐ Ⓑ Ⓒ Ⓓ Ⓔ	25. Ⓐ Ⓑ Ⓒ Ⓓ Ⓔ

Writing Sample

Schools would like to get to know you better through a story you tell using one of the ideas below. Please choose the idea you find most interesting and write a story using the idea as your first sentence. Please fill in the circle next to the one you choose.

(A) If you could relive a particular moment, what would it be and why?

(B) She looked up and gasped.

Use this page and the next page to complete your writing sample.

Continue on next page

SECTION 1

25 Questions

Following each problem in this section, there are five suggested answers. Work out each problem in your head or in the blank space provided at the right of the page. Then look at the five suggested answers and decide which one is best.

Note: Figures that accompany problems in this section are drawn as accurately as possible EXCEPT when it is stated in a specific problem that its figure is not drawn to scale.

Sample problem:

5,413	(A) 586
− 4,827	(B) 596
	(C) 696
	(D) 1,586
	(E) 1,686

● Ⓑ Ⓒ Ⓓ Ⓔ

USE THIS SPACE FOR FIGURING.

1. When 9206 is divided by 180, the remainder is

   (A) 26

   (B) 39

   (C) 42

   (D) 51

   (E) 56

---

2. $3/4 + 0.34 =$

   (A) 0.34

   (B) 0.43

   (C) 0.68

   (D) 1.09

   (E) 2.68

GO ON TO THE NEXT PAGE.

3. Which of the following is a whole number?

    (A) –2.5

    (B) $106/3$

    (C) 33%

    (D) $108/3$

    (E) 1.25

4. In the figure to the right, two congruent regular pentagons are joined at the base. If the perimeter of the entire figure is 40, each pentagon must have a side length of

    (A) 4

    (B) 5

    (C) 8

    (D) 10

    (E) 16

5. According to the graph to the right, what were the approximate average earnings of the three highest-grossing films during the weekend of July 13-15?

    (A) $20 million

    (B) $30 million

    (C) $40 million

    (D) $50 million

    (E) $80 million

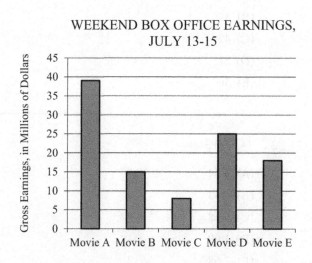

WEEKEND BOX OFFICE EARNINGS, JULY 13-15

GO ON TO THE NEXT PAGE.

6. If $N \div 2 = 14$, then $N \div 4 =$

    (A) 2
    (B) 6
    (C) 7
    (D) 14
    (E) 28

---

7. $\dfrac{1}{4}\left(\dfrac{1}{2}\right) + \dfrac{1}{16} =$

    (A) $^1/_{32}$

    (B) $^2/_{16}$

    (C) $^3/_{16}$

    (D) $^2/_8$

    (E) $^1/_2$

---

8. If $N + 2 > 2$, then which of the following MUST be true?

    (A) $N > 0$
    (B) $N + 1 < 2$
    (C) $N + 1 > 2$
    (D) $N > 1$
    (E) $N = 2$

---

9. A train took between $2\dfrac{1}{4}$ and $2\dfrac{1}{2}$ hours to complete a 150 mile trip. What was the train's average speed, in miles per hour?

    (A) 50
    (B) 59
    (C) 62
    (D) 67
    (E) 75

GO ON TO THE NEXT PAGE.

10. How many small cubes with a side length of 1 meter can fit in a larger cube with a side length of 5 meters?

    (A) 5

    (B) 10

    (C) 25

    (D) 125

    (E) 200

---

11. Ms. Jarwahl owns one apartment that measures 60 feet by 40 feet. She also owns a second apartment that measures 30 feet by 90 feet. What is the average square footage of the two apartments?

    (A) 2400 ft^2

    (B) 2450 ft^2

    (C) 2550 ft^2

    (D) 2700 ft^2

    (E) 3200 ft^2

---

12. Which of the following numbers can be written in the form $7C + 2$, if C is an integer?

    (A) 36

    (B) 44

    (C) 52

    (D) 60

    (E) 68

---

13. Kathy has replaced all of her incandescent light bulbs with fluorescent light bulbs that last 8 times longer. Compared with how frequently Kathy had to change her incandescent light bulbs previously, she will now have to change her new light bulbs

    (A) 8% as frequently

    (B) 12.5% as frequently

    (C) 15% as frequently

    (D) 80% as frequently

    (E) 92% as frequently

GO ON TO THE NEXT PAGE.

14. If one fourth of the height of a giraffe is 5 ft., three fifths of the giraffe's height is

    (A) 4 ft.

    (B) 5 ft.

    (C) 8 ft.

    (D) 10 ft.

    (E) 12 ft.

15. Which of the following shapes can be drawn without re-tracing or lifting your pencil?

    A)

    (B)

    (C)

    (D)

    (E)

16. Harvey has a loan of $1,000, for which he pays about $9.88 in interest every month. This monthly interest is $1/12$ of his yearly interest. What is Harvey's yearly interest rate on his $1,000 loan?

    (A) 0.83%

    (B) 4.62%

    (C) 9.88%

    (D) 10.98%

    (E) 11.86%

GO ON TO THE NEXT PAGE.

17. In the figure to the right, two parallel lines are intersected by a third line. If $x = 110$, what is the value of y?

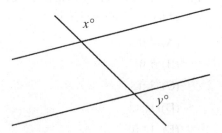

    (A) 60

    (B) 70

    (C) 80

    (D) 10

    (E) It cannot be determined from the information given.

18. To share the cost of a gift equally, three people would each have to contribute $4. If five friends decided to share the cost of this gift equally, how much would each friend need to contribute?

    (A) $1.00

    (B) $2.00

    (C) $2.25

    (D) $2.40

    (E) $4.00

19. Quynh acquires 3 rugs, 4 tapestries, and 6 candelabras to decorate her castle. If she places one of each item in the grand hall, how many possible combinations of rug-tapestry-candelabra are there remaining for her bedchamber?

    (A) 85

    (B) 80

    (C) 72

    (D) 48

    (E) 30

GO ON TO THE NEXT PAGE.

20. Points A, B, C, D, and E lie along a straight line, in that order. The distance between A and B is 5, and the distance between C and E is 4. The distance between B and D is 2. If the distance between A and E is 10, what is the distance between A and C?

    (A) 1
    (B) 2
    (C) 4
    (D) 5
    (E) 6

---

21. $$(3x + 2)\,(x - 3)$$

    Which of the following is equivalent to the expression above?

    (A) $3x^2 - 7x + 6$
    (B) $3x^2 + 7x + 6$
    (C) $3x^2 + 3x - 1$
    (D) $3x^2 - x + 6$
    (E) $3x^2 - 7x - 6$

---

22. The organizers of a relay race are sending 3 buses to pick up runners and take them to the race site. There are 3 runners on each team, and all members of each team must travel together on the same bus. If each bus can seat 20 runners, then how many total teams can fit into the 3 buses?

    (A) 15
    (B) 16
    (C) 18
    (D) 20
    (E) 21

23. $$AB + C6 = DE0$$

Each of the five letters in the equation above stands for one of the following digits: 1, 2, 4, 5, and 6. If each letter stands for a different digit, which letter stands for the digit 2?

(A) A

(B) B

(C) C

(D) D

(E) E

24. Total sales, s, is proportional to the number of goods sold, n, and a constant price, p. Which of the following correctly represents the value of n in terms of s and p?

(A) $n = {}^s/_p$

(B) $n = {}^p/_s$

(C) $p = {}^n/_s$

(D) $p = ns$

(E) $n = sp$

25. If Line A is parallel to another line with the equation $2y - 4 = 12x$, what is the slope of Line A?

(A) -4

(B) 6

(C) 8

(D) 12

(E) 24

STOP

IF YOU FINISH BEFORE TIME IS CALLED,
YOU MAY CHECK YOUR WORK ON THIS SECTION ONLY.
DO NOT TURN TO ANY OTHER SECTION IN THE TEST.

Read each passage carefully and then answer the questions about it. For each question, decide on the basis of the passage which one of the choices best answers the question.

There they sat, nearly thirty of them, on the rough benches, their faces shading from a pale cream to a deep brown, the little feet bare and swinging, the eyes full of expectation, with here and there a twinkle of mischief, and the hands grasping Webster's blue-back spelling-book. I loved my school, and the fine faith the children had in my wisdom as their teacher was truly marvelous. We read
Line 5 and spelled together, wrote a little, picked flowers, sang, and listened to stories of the world beyond the hill. At times the school would dwindle away, and I would start out. I would visit the Eddings, who lived in two very dirty rooms, and ask why little Lugene, whose flaming face seemed ever ablaze with the dark-red hair uncombed, was absent all last week, or why the unmistakable rags of Mack and Ed were so often missing. Then their father would tell me how the crops needed the boys, and their mother
10 would assure me that Lugene must mind the baby. "But we'll start them again next week." When the Lawrences stopped, I knew that the doubts of the old folks about book-learning had conquered again, and so, toiling up the hill, I put Cicero's "pro Archia Poeta" into the simplest English, and usually convinced them—for a week or so.

1. How did the speaker feel about his job at the school?

    (A) He enjoyed having such easy and entertaining work.
    (B) He resented the fact that his students didn't appreciate his expertise.
    (C) He was bored by the simple activities he had to engage in with his students.
    (D) He was proud of his school and worked hard to maintain it.
    (E) He was tired and eager to quit.

2. According to the passage, when school attendance was low the speaker would

    (A) pay social calls to while away the time
    (B) visit his students' families to find out why they were missing school
    (C) read British poetry to his students in their homes
    (D) entertain his students and their families with stories about history
    (E) recruit new students

GO ON TO THE NEXT PAGE.

3. What reasons do the Eddings give for their children's absence from school?

 (A) The children are being kept home as a punishment.

 (B) The children are needed at home to help with the farm and family.

 (C) The parents don't want their children to be seen by their classmates.

 (D) The parents don't want their children to become more educated.

 (E) The children don't enjoy school and prefer to stay home.

4. It can be inferred from the passage that Cicero's "pro Archia Poeta" (line 12) is

 (A) a Latin treatise about farming

 (B) a short story describing the benefits of studying geography

 (C) a homework assignment that the speaker's students had not completed

 (D) a poem about the uneducated

 (E) not written in simple English

GO ON TO THE NEXT PAGE.

The following is an excerpt from a speech by former United States President Lyndon B. Johnson.

Each year more than 100,000 high school graduates, with proved ability, do not enter college because they cannot afford it. And if we cannot educate today's youth, what will we do in 1970 when elementary school enrollment will be 5 million greater than 1960?

In many places, classrooms are overcrowded and curricula are outdated. Most of our qualified
Line 5 teachers are underpaid, and many of our paid teachers are unqualified. So we must give every child a place to sit and a teacher to learn from. Poverty must not be a bar to learning, and learning must offer an escape from poverty.

But more classrooms and more teachers are not enough. We must seek an educational system which grows in excellence as it grows in size. This means better training for our
10 teachers. It means preparing youth to enjoy their hours of leisure as well as their hours of labor. It means exploring new techniques of teaching, to find new ways to stimulate the love of learning and the capacity for creation.

5. What is the main message of this passage?

(A) We must replace poor teachers with better ones.

(B) Poverty is a serious problem in today's society.

(C) We must improve the educational system.

(D) There are too many children in the educational system.

(E) Teaching is a very difficult career.

6. This passage was most likely written

(A) in 1940
(B) in 1950
(C) in 1960
(D) in 1970
(E) in 1980

7. The speaker identifies all of the following as problems for the educational system, EXCEPT:

(A) the rising cost of early-childhood education

(B) overcrowding in schools

(C) low pay for teachers

(D) the high cost of a college education

(E) curricula that contain out-of-date information

8. When the speaker says "poverty must not be a bar to learning" (line 6), he is implying that

(A) poverty is like a ruler that measures potential in school

(B) impoverished students have fewer educational opportunities

(C) poverty has no effect on education

(D) impoverished families live too far away from schools

(E) poverty is the primary reason that students have unqualified teachers

GO ON TO THE NEXT PAGE.

9. The speaker would most likely agree that

   (A) not everyone should attend college

   (B) most teachers lack qualifications

   (C) hiring more teachers will solve all of the problems in the education system

   (D) students should work harder in school

   (E) children learn better when they enjoy learning

10. The tone of the passage is

   (A) condescending

   (B) mournful

   (C) wrathful

   (D) emphatic

   (E) sarcastic

GO ON TO THE NEXT PAGE.

Sometimes geography can affect language in surprising ways.

On the island of La Gomera—one of the Canary Islands off the cost of West Africa—deep ravines separate slivers of mountain terrain and the people who live on it. But the inhabitants of La Gomera developed a unique way of communicating across these deep ravines: an amazing whistled speech called Silbo Gomero. This whistled language is indigenous to the island, and its existence has been documented since Roman times. Invented by the original inhabitants of the island, the Guanches, Silbo Gomero was adopted by the Spanish settlers in the 16th century and survived after the Guanches' population dwindled. When this unique means of communication was threatened with extinction at the dawn of the 21st century, the local government added it to the school curriculum.

Line 5

10

The modern language of Silbo Gomero is actually a dialect of Spanish. The Guanches originally converted the sounds of their own language into whistle-sounds, but eventually applied that practice to the language of the Spanish colonists. It is this whistled language that the Spaniards themselves adopted.

11. The primary subject of this passage is

(A) the geography of La Gomera

(B) the Spanish occupation of the Canary Islands

(C) geography's relationship to language

(D) Silbo Gomero, the whistled language of La Gomera

(E) languages that involve whistling and other non-vocal sounds

12. According to the passage, Silbo Gomero

I.   is at least as old as the Roman Empire

II. has evolved into a whistled dialect of Spanish

III. has been taught in schools in La Gomera

(A) I only

(B) II only

(C) III only

(D) I and II only

(E) I, II and III

13. Silbo Gomero was developed by the inhabitants of La Gomera so they could

(A) plot against the Spanish colonists

(B) communicate better in their terrain

(C) communicate with Spanish settlers

(D) enhance La Gomera's unique culture

(E) communicate more privately with one another

14. How did the Spanish acquire Silbo Gomero?

(A) They learned it in the schools of La Gomera.

(B) They were the original settlers of La Gomera and invented the language.

(C) They converted the Guanches' whistle sounds into their own Spanish language.

(D) They picked up the whistled form of Spanish that the Guanches had invented.

(E) They began whistling in order to communicate better with the Guanches.

GO ON TO THE NEXT PAGE.

15. It can be inferred that La Gomera's ravines

    (A) were detrimental to the family units of La Gomera

    (B) helped give rise to a new language

    (C) caused conflict among the inhabitants

    (D) confused the Spanish colonists

    (E) developed after people settled on La Gomera

GO ON TO THE NEXT PAGE.

Children have the strangest adventures without being troubled by them. For instance, they may remember to mention, a week after the event happened, that when they were in the wood they had met their dead father and played a game with him. It was in this casual way that Wendy one morning made a worrying revelation. Some leaves of a tree had been found on the nursery floor, which certainly

Line 5   were not there when the children went to bed, and Mrs. Darling was puzzling over them when Wendy said with a tolerant smile:

"I do believe it is that Peter again!"

"Whatever do you mean, Wendy?"

"It is so naughty of him not to wipe his feet," Wendy said, sighing. She was a tidy child.

10   She explained in quite a matter-of-fact way that she thought Peter sometimes came to the nursery in the night and sat on the foot of her bed and played on his pipes to her. Unfortunately she never woke, so she didn't know how she knew, she just knew.

"What nonsense you talk, precious. No one can get into the house without knocking."

"I think he comes in by the window," she said.

15   "My love, it is three floors up."

"Were not the leaves at the foot of the window, mother?"

It was quite true; the leaves had been found very near the window.

Mrs. Darling did not know what to think, for it all seemed so natural to Wendy that you could not dismiss it by saying she had been dreaming.

20   "My child," the mother cried, "why did you not tell me of this before?"

"I forgot," said Wendy lightly. She was in a hurry to get her breakfast.

Oh, surely she must have been dreaming.

16. According to the passage, Wendy believes that Peter

(A) is her father
(B) is a character in a book
(C) is responsible for the leaves on the floor
(D) knocks on the front door every night
(E) eats breakfast with her every morning

17. Mrs. Darling could best be described as

(A) erudite
(B) severe
(C) perplexed
(D) gullible
(E) anguished

18. Wendy's attitude towards Peter could be described as

(A) frankly astonished
(B) mildly exasperated
(C) secretly frightened
(D) quietly proud
(E) absolutely smitten

19. Without changing the author's meaning, you could replace the word "natural" (line 18) with which of the following words?

(A) woodsy
(B) carefree
(C) normal
(D) unavoidable
(E) complicated

GO ON TO THE NEXT PAGE.

20. The narrator would most likely agree with
    which of the following statements?

    (A) Children tend to exaggerate.

    (B) Children often perceive imaginary
        events as real.

    (C) Children frequently play tricks on their
        parents.

    (D) Children have a faulty and undeveloped
        memory.

    (E) Children's dreams are sporadic.

GO ON TO THE NEXT PAGE.

A green leaf is green because of the presence of a pigment known as chlorophyll, but chlorophyll is not the only pigment in a leaf. Leaves also contain carotenoids, yellow and orange pigments that are present in the leaf throughout its life, and anthocyanins, red and purple pigments that develop under certain conditions in the late summer. As long as the leaf

Line 5 has plenty of chlorophyll, green will be the dominant color.

Chlorophyll has a vital function: it captures solar rays and utilizes the resulting energy to manufacture the plant's food—simple sugars that are produced from water and carbon dioxide gas and are the sole source of the carbohydrates the plant needs for growth and development. Throughout the spring and summer, the plant continually replenishes the

10 chlorophyll in its leaves so that they can keep producing its food.

In late summer, as daylight hours shorten and temperatures cool, the veins that carry fluids into and out of the leaf are gradually closed off as a layer of special cork cells forms at the base of each leaf. As this cork layer develops, the flow of chlorophyll into the leaf decreases, slowly at first, and then rapidly. Eventually, the flow of the replacement

15 chlorophyll cannot keep pace with the rate at which the chlorophyll is used up, and the leaf begins to change colors. Without the chlorophyll there to mask them, the yellow, orange, red and purple colors of the other leaf-pigments begin to show through.

21. According to the passage, chlorophyll is responsible for

   I.   all pigmentation in a plant's leaves
   II. processing solar energy to create the plant's food
   III. converting a plant's carbon dioxide into water

   (A) I only
   (B) II only
   (C) II and III only
   (D) I and III only
   (E) I, II, and III

22. According to the passage, a leaf's supply of chlorophyll is replenished by

   (A) the formation of cork cells at the base of each leaf
   (B) water condensation from the atmosphere
   (C) the production of carbohydrates
   (D) veins that transport fluids into each leaf
   (E) solar rays

23. Red, yellow, and purple leaf pigments reveal themselves

   (A) during the process of photosynthesis
   (B) on cloudy days
   (C) when a leaf needs carbon dioxide
   (D) when a leaf has more chlorophyll
   (E) when a leaf has less chlorophyll

GO ON TO THE NEXT PAGE.

24. To what question might this passage be the answer?

   (A) What are the functions of chlorophyll, carotenoids and anthocyanins?

   (B) How do plants feed themselves?

   (C) Why are leaves green, and why do they change color?

   (D) What causes the seasons to change?

   (E) Why are some trees always green?

25. According to the passage, carotenoids produce which of the following colors?

   (A) yellow and orange

   (B) green

   (C) red and purple

   (D) yellow and purple

   (E) orange and red

GO ON TO THE NEXT PAGE.

It may be misery not to sing at all
And to go silent through the brimming day.
It may be sorrow never to be loved,
But deeper griefs than these beset the way.

Line 5   To have come near to sing the perfect song
And only by a half-tone lost the key,
There is the potent sorrow, there the grief,
The pale, sad staring of life's tragedy.

This, this it is to be accursed indeed;
10   For if we mortals love, or if we sing,
We count our joys not by the things we have,
But by what kept us from the perfect thing.

26. Which of these best sums up the main idea of the poem?

(A) It is better to have loved and lost than never to have loved at all.

(B) Life's greatest sorrow is to come near to a great thing and never reach it.

(C) Perfection in everything is the speaker's one ambition.

(D) Happy is the person who can be content without love.

(E) Life's greatest joy is to find true love, because true love lasts forever.

27. Throughout the poem, the speaker compares love to

(A) a bird

(B) immortality

(C) a tragedy

(D) singing

(E) perfection

28. The tone of this poem could be described as

(A) cynical

(B) reflective

(C) morose

(D) angry

(E) contemptuous

29. Based on the speaker's opinion in the poem, which of these would be worse than never pursuing a desire to become a painter?

(A) being a very good painter, but not quite a great painter

(B) becoming a singer instead

(C) painting every day, but keeping your paintings to yourself

(D) having your paintings praised by others, but not liking them yourself

(E) never pursuing a love interest

GO ON TO THE NEXT PAGE.

Wireless reports this evening indicate that the Cunarder Carpathia reached the position from which distress calls were sent out by the Titanic last night after her collision with an iceberg. The Carpathia found there the remains and lifeboats of what had been the largest steamship in service.

The sinking of the Titanic occurred at about 2:20a.m. All her boats have been found and around

Line 5　655 survivors have been rescued. About 2,100 crew members and passengers were traveling on the Titanic.

While the Leyland liner California continues to search the location of the wreckage, the Carpathia is bringing the survivors back to New York.

News of the disaster was first received 10:25 last night by wireless, and the ship continued to

10　signal until a last blurred signal was sent and ended abruptly at 12:27a.m. Until that time, the operator's signals were perfectly clear and steady. He remained level-headed throughout and exercised the best possible judgment.

30. It can be inferred from the passage that the Olympic, the Carpathia, and the California are

(A) icebergs

(B) helicopters

(C) rescue workers

(D) ships

(E) hotels

31. This passage would most likely be found in

(A) an encyclopedia

(B) a memoir

(C) a newspaper

(D) a film script

(E) a letter

32. The "boats" mentioned in line 4 are probably

(A) lifeboats used to rescue the passengers and crew

(B) rescue boats from the Carpathia

(C) fishing boats from the surrounding area

(D) armed boats that defended the Titanic

(E) the Olympic, the Carpathia, and the California

33. According to the passage, all of the following is true EXCEPT:

(A) the last signals from the Titanic were received not long after midnight

(B) the Leyland liner California returned to New York with all the survivors

(C) at the time of writing, about 1,445 people from aboard the ship were unaccounted for

(D) the Titanic wired calls for help starting at 10:25 p.m.

(E) the Titanic sank at about 2:20 a.m.

GO ON TO THE NEXT PAGE.

34. The passage's tone when describing the Titanic's wireless operator (lines 9-11) suggests that the author considers him to be

(A) foolish

(B) unkind

(C) ignorant

(D) admirable

(E) generous

Henri Marie Raymond de Toulouse-Lautrec-Monfa—or more simply, Henri de Toulouse-Lautrec—was a French painter and illustrator whose immersion in the colorful life of Paris in the last decades of the 19th century yielded a collection of exciting, elegant and provocative images. Henri owed his long name to his aristocratic heritage, to which he also owed his serious life-long health problems. Henri's parents, the Count and Countess of
Line 5 Toulouse and Lautrec, were first cousins, and Henri suffered from health conditions often found in the offspring of close relatives. At the age of 13, Henri fractured his right thigh bone, and at 14, his left. The breaks did not heal properly, and his legs ceased to grow, so that as an adult he was just over five feet tall, having developed an adult-sized torso while retaining his child-sized legs. Physically unable to participate in many activities typically enjoyed by men of his age, Henri immersed himself in art.

10 Under the tutelage of Bonnat and later Fernand Cormon, Henri developed his vivid, characterful painting style and his taste for the Paris social scene that was so often his subject. He was masterly at capturing crowd scenes in which the figures are highly individualized. Along with Cézanne, Van Gogh, and Gauguin, Henri Toulouse-Lautrec is now known as one of the greatest painters of the period.

35. Based on the description in the passage, the paintings of Henri de Toulouse-Lautrec are most likely

(A) drab
(B) abstract
(C) visionary
(D) satirical
(E) vibrant

36. The author states that Henri's long name and physical ailments were both a result of

(A) malnutrition as a child
(B) his talent as a painter
(C) his lack of athletic ability
(D) his aristocratic origins
(E) his imaginative parents

37. The author suggests that Henri's masterpieces

(A) were inspired by his engagement in the social life of his city
(B) were successful due to his family's influence
(C) cured him of his disabilities
(D) allowed him to keep living the life of an aristocrat
(E) surpassed his family's low expectations

38. According to the passage, Henri's health problems

(A) forced him to become an artist because there were no other careers open to him
(B) prevented him from enjoying certain experiences with his peers
(C) directly caused his death
(D) were common among artists in Paris during this period
(E) raised his social status

GO ON TO THE NEXT PAGE.

39. Which of the following does the author consider one of Henri's greatest strengths as a painter?

(A) his inspiring biography

(B) his innovative use of color and texture

(C) his ability to provoke a viewer's imagination through his illustrations

(D) his memorable appearance

(E) his ability to portray individual people within a crowd

40. Based on the information in the passage, Fernand Comon was most likely

(A) one of Henri's childhood friends

(B) an art critic

(C) one of Henri's relatives

(D) an art teacher

(E) Henri's patron

STOP

IF YOU FINISH BEFORE TIME IS CALLED,
YOU MAY CHECK YOUR WORK ON THIS SECTION ONLY.
DO NOT TURN TO ANY OTHER SECTION IN THE TEST.

SECTION 3
60 Questions

This section consists of two different types of questions: synonyms and analogies. There are directions and a sample question for each type.

Synonyms

Each of the following questions consists of one word followed by five words or phrases. You are to select the one word or phrase whose meaning is closest to the word in capital letters.

Sample Question:

CHILLY:

(A) lazy
(B) nice
(C) dry
(D) cold
(E) sunny

---

1. EVADE:

    (A) depart
    (B) defend
    (C) escape
    (D) dislike
    (E) descend

2. SPRUCE:

    (A) broom
    (B) cleanliness
    (C) virtue
    (D) flavor
    (E) evergreen

3. FRIVOLOUS:

    (A) enjoyable
    (B) silly
    (C) outrageous
    (D) unseemly
    (E) unkempt

4. PARTRIDGE:

    (A) musical score
    (B) wood fowl
    (C) ripe fruit
    (D) wreath
    (E) mountaintop

5. DEDUCE:

    (A) lessen
    (B) tutor
    (C) demote
    (D) decline
    (E) infer

6. APPLICABLE:

    (A) submissive
    (B) appropriate
    (C) open
    (D) apprehensive
    (E) handy

GO ON TO THE NEXT PAGE.

Practice Tests

7. VOLUNTEER:

   (A) offer

   (B) undergo

   (C) gift

   (D) chatter

   (E) limit

8. FROLIC:

   (A) hike

   (B) disembark

   (C) cavort

   (D) hoodwink

   (E) inundate

9. SYNCHRONIZE:

   (A) wind

   (B) record

   (C) measure

   (D) unify

   (E) color

10. CRUDE:

   (A) naked

   (B) insolent

   (C) unrefined

   (D) colorful

   (E) exacting

11. APPREHEND:

   (A) charge

   (B) sentence

   (C) handcuff

   (D) understand

   (E) photograph

12. JUVENILE:

   (A) imprisoned

   (B) green

   (C) joyful

   (D) innovative

   (E) healthy

13. WIRED:

   (A) crackling

   (B) catered

   (C) remote

   (D) excited

   (E) summoned

14. ANTAGONIZE:

   (A) bury a relative

   (B) celebrate a holiday

   (C) crush an insect

   (D) introduce a theme

   (E) make an enemy

15. REGENERATION:

   (A) denial

   (B) agreement

   (C) great-great-grandparents

   (D) restoration

   (E) recrimination

16. HEEDLESS:

   (A) hungry

   (B) open

   (C) reckless

   (D) remorseless

   (E) headstrong

GO ON TO THE NEXT PAGE.

17. ASSIMILATE:

   (A) anticipate

   (B) reject

   (C) incorporate

   (D) raise

   (E) return

18. REGIMEN:

   (A) plan

   (B) team

   (C) election

   (D) hunger

   (E) argument

19. ASSENT:

   (A) justify

   (B) prove

   (C) cultivate

   (D) approve

   (E) ponder

20. SKULK:

   (A) sneak

   (B) cry

   (C) blossom

   (D) run

   (E) swim

21. ABHOR:

   (A) tend

   (B) expel

   (C) criticize

   (D) loathe

   (E) demean

22. IRASCIBLE:

   (A) grumpy

   (B) unstylish

   (C) immoral

   (D) motivated

   (E) insane

23. TROUNCE:

   (A) denounce

   (B) rout

   (C) fish

   (D) captivate

   (E) capture

24. BRAND:

   (A) oats

   (B) finance

   (C) bravery

   (D) store

   (E) mark

25. RENDITION:

   (A) refrain

   (B) article

   (C) version

   (D) song

   (E) collection

26. INSIPID:

   (A) dull

   (B) tasty

   (C) liquid

   (D) invasive

   (E) isolated

GO ON TO THE NEXT PAGE.

27. ONEROUS:

    (A) exceedingly difficult

    (B) constantly rowdy

    (C) very decisive

    (D) completely united

    (E) entirely mythical

28. HOIST:

    (A) drop

    (B) plow

    (C) lift

    (D) strain

    (E) lever

29. HEAP:

    (A) compost

    (B) roll

    (C) rake

    (D) bury

    (E) pile

30. LIVID:

    (A) vivacious

    (B) life-long

    (C) disappointed

    (D) furious

    (E) verbose

GO ON TO THE NEXT PAGE.

Analogies

The following questions ask you to find relationships between words. For each question, select the answer choice that best completes the meaning of the sentence.

Sample Question:

> Kitten is to cat as
>
> (A) fawn is to colt
> (B) puppy is to dog
> (C) cow is to bull
> (D) wolf is to bear
> (E) hen is to rooster

Choice (B) is the best answer because a kitten is a young cat just as a puppy is a young dog. Of all the answer choices, (B) states a relationship that is most like the relationship between kitten and cat.

---

31. Scissors are to paper as

    (A) string is to box
    (B) glue is to clippings
    (C) knife is to butter
    (D) hatchet is to lumberjack
    (E) pencil is to sharpener

32. Gum is to stick as

    (A) wad is to money
    (B) ice is to cube
    (C) spice is to taste
    (D) bubble is to branch
    (E) chocolate is to wrapper

33. Pathetic is to pity as awesome is to

    (A) warmth
    (B) pride
    (C) cool
    (D) boredom
    (E) amazement

34. Inter is to tomb as

    (A) steeple is to cathedral
    (B) shroud is to mourn
    (C) bury is to body
    (D) deposit is to bank
    (E) interval is to entomb

35. Dam is to river as

    (A) speculation is to concept
    (B) reckoning is to analysis
    (C) filibuster is to vote
    (D) analysis is to confusion
    (E) mother is to bay

36. Hour is to watch as

    (A) pound is to scale
    (B) minute is to second
    (C) hourglass is to clock
    (D) thermometer is to fever
    (E) day is to year

GO ON TO THE NEXT PAGE.

Practice Tests

37. Wind is to whistle as

    (A) hum is to heaven

    (B) brook is to babble

    (C) leaf is to laugh

    (D) grass is to giggle

    (E) shore is to shout

38. Doctor is to health as

    (A) actor is to theater

    (B) cartoonist is to funny

    (C) personal trainer is to fitness

    (D) philosopher is to truth

    (E) plumber is to toilet

39. Cross is to angry as

    (A) droll is to funny

    (B) dull is to smiling

    (C) firm is to feeble

    (D) young is to touchy

    (E) healthy is to agreeable

40. Vivacious is to lively as

    (A) fertile is to pretty

    (B) loquacious is to talkative

    (C) gargantuan is to cheerful

    (D) insane is to normal

    (E) tranquil is to wild

41. Ravioli is to dumpling as

    (A) taco is to shell

    (B) rice is to soup

    (C) chocolate is to cake

    (D) mint is to lollipop

    (E) spaghetti is to noodle

42. Gravity is to force as

    (A) levity is to humorous

    (B) oxygen is to element

    (C) pathogen is to illness

    (D) electricity is to magnetism

    (E) hearing is to vibration

43. Impound is to property as

    (A) impersonate is to officer

    (B) imprison is to person

    (C) profound is to theory

    (D) resounding is to success

    (E) employ is to subordinate

44. Password is to account as

    (A) identity is to individual

    (B) number is to phone

    (C) bank is to secret

    (D) watchword is to lookout

    (E) key is to house

45. Insolence is to brazen as

    (A) rebellion is to cautious

    (B) obedience is to dutiful

    (C) insulin is to sugar

    (D) contempt is to submission

    (E) humble is to servant

46. Careless is to neglect as

    (A) sloppy is to work

    (B) untidy is to workplace

    (C) cruel is to punishment

    (D) malicious is to sabotage

    (E) objective is to plan

GO ON TO THE NEXT PAGE.

47. Inhospitable is to welcoming as unbearable is to

   (A) colorful
   (B) picturesque
   (C) lamentable
   (D) enjoyable
   (E) ridiculous

48. Utopia is to location as

   (A) European is to continental
   (B) euphoria is to sensation
   (C) unified is to disparate
   (D) enthusiastic is to salutation
   (E) myopia is to place

49. Caricature is to person as

   (A) parody is to artwork
   (B) criticism is to movie
   (C) derision is to joke
   (D) rejection is to offer
   (E) admiration is to hero

50. Tie is to neck as

   (A) seatbelt is to car
   (B) shoe is to lace
   (C) coat is to arm
   (D) sash is to waist
   (E) button is to shirt

51. Varied is to identical as

   (A) collaborative is to unilateral
   (B) reticent is to hesitant
   (C) joyous is to serious
   (D) mysterious is to friendly
   (E) exotic is to alike

52. Hibernate is to nap as

   (A) den is to bedroom
   (B) sun is to moon
   (C) gorge is to nibble
   (D) some are to all
   (E) spontaneous is to temporary

53. Effervescent is to bubbles as

   (A) courageous is to fire
   (B) expedient is to embers
   (C) curtailed is to seeds
   (D) reminiscent is to roses
   (E) scintillating is to sparkles

54. Recall is to memory as

   (A) ignore is to feeling
   (B) connect is to meeting
   (C) listen is to anecdote
   (D) suppose is to speculation
   (E) pursue is to dream

55. Excavate is to dig as

   (A) investigate is to listen
   (B) evacuate is to empty
   (C) control is to order
   (D) discover is to mystify
   (E) orient is to map

56. Cactus is to plant as

   (A) snake is to reptile
   (B) necklace is to jewelry
   (C) porcupine is to animal
   (D) hydrangea is to flower
   (E) amethyst is to gem

GO ON TO THE NEXT PAGE.

57. Plutocrat is to opulent as

   (A) farmer is to farming

   (B) messenger is to swift

   (C) democrat is to democracy

   (D) soldier is to salutary

   (E) beggar is to destitute

58. Palatial is to space as

   (A) labyrinthine is to corridors

   (B) somber is to mood

   (C) character is to morality

   (D) insomniac is to sleep

   (E) sorry is to wrong

59. Problem is to calamity as

   (A) happiness is to cheer

   (B) luck is to veracity

   (C) meal is to banquet

   (D) discovery is to calumny

   (E) animosity is to dislike

60. Pugnacious is to fight as

   (A) gluttonous is to eat

   (B) voracious is to read

   (C) contagious is to vomit

   (D) courageous is to succeed

   (E) compatible is to compete

STOP

IF YOU FINISH BEFORE TIME IS CALLED,
YOU MAY CHECK YOUR WORK ON THIS SECTION ONLY.
DO NOT TURN TO ANY OTHER SECTION IN THE TEST.

Following each problem in this section, there are five suggested answers. Work out each problem in your head or in the blank space provided at the right of the page. Then look at the five suggested answers and decide which one is best.

Note: Figures that accompany problems in this section are drawn as accurately as possible EXCEPT when it is stated in a specific problem that its figure is not drawn to scale.

Sample problem:

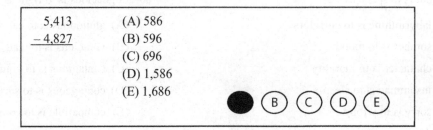

5,413
− 4,827

(A) 586
(B) 596
(C) 696
(D) 1,586
(E) 1,686

USE THIS SPACE FOR FIGURING.

1. John has x erasers more than Ed. If Ed has 10 erasers, how many erasers does John have?

   A $10x$

   B $x + 10$

   C $10 - x$

   D $10 \div x$

   E   10

2. The quotient of 63 divided by 7 is

   (A) 6

   (B) 7

   (C) 8

   (D) 9

   (E) 63

GO ON TO THE NEXT PAGE.

3. Ariel has $7.75 and Javier has $10.25. How much money does Javier need to give Ariel for each to have the same amount?

   (A) $0.75
   (B) $1.25
   (C) $1.75
   (D) $2.50
   (E) $9.00

4. $\frac{1}{4} + \frac{4}{1} =$

   (A) $\frac{4}{5}$
   (B) $\frac{5}{5}$
   (C) $\frac{5}{4}$
   (D) 4
   (E) $\frac{17}{4}$

5. 3.562 is closest in value to

   (A) 3.526
   (B) 3.560
   (C) 3.563
   (D) 3.625
   (E) 3.652

6. 12 is 5 percent of

   (A) 0.6
   (B) 6
   (C) 24
   (D) 60
   (E) 240

GO ON TO THE NEXT PAGE.

7. In the figure to the right, what is the value of z?

    (A) 40°

    (B) 45°

    (C) 70°

    (D) 110°

    (E) 135°

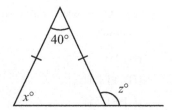

8. If $0.25 \times N = 4N$, then $N=$

    (A) 0

    (B) 1

    (C) 4

    (D) 16

    (E) It cannot be determined from the information given.

9. A T-shirt is on sale for 25% off of the regular price of $15.99. About how much less is the sale price than the regular price?

    (A) $3

    (B) $4

    (C) $8

    (D) $9

    (E) $12

10. Mr. Bouchard is building fences around two rectangular fields. One field measures 120 feet by 200 feet, and the other field measures 160 feet by 100 feet. If the two fields are not adjacent, how many feet of fencing will Mr. Bouchard need to surround both fields?

    (A) 900

    (B) 1050

    (C) 1100

    (D) 1160

    (E) 1200

GO ON TO THE NEXT PAGE.

11. If $\frac{2}{3} + M < \frac{1}{6}$, which of the following could be a value for M?

(A) $-\frac{2}{3}$

(B) $-\frac{1}{2}$

(C) $-\frac{1}{3}$

(D) $\frac{1}{3}$

(E) $\frac{2}{3}$

12. Gabrielle has packed 15 pieces of clothing for a vacation, but has only $\frac{3}{4}$ of the clothes she will need. How many more pieces of clothing does she need to pack?

(A) 5

(B) 6

(C) 7

(D) 8

(E) 9

13. According to the graph to the right, pencil production increased at the greatest rate between which years?

(A) 1990-1994

(B) 1994-1998

(C) 1998-2002

(D) 2002-2006

(E) 2006-2010

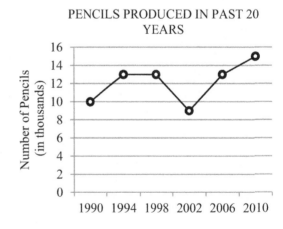

PENCILS PRODUCED IN PAST 20 YEARS

GO ON TO THE NEXT PAGE.

14. The sum of three consecutive odd integers is 27. What is the smallest of the three integers?

    (A) 3
    (B) 5
    (C) 7
    (D) 11
    (E) 15

15. Cindy is 4 years older than Sally, and Sally is twice as old as Nicole. If Cindy is 18, how old is Nicole?

    (A) 4
    (B) 7
    (C) 9
    (D) 11
    (E) 14

16. In a school picnic, a total of 43 students brought a backpack, a lunchbox, or both a backpack and a lunchbox. If there are a total of 23 backpacks and 25 lunchboxes, how many students brought both a backpack and a lunchbox?

    (A) 5
    (B) 7
    (C) 10
    (D) 17
    (E) 20

GO ON TO THE NEXT PAGE.

Questions 17 and 18 refer to the following definition.

For all real numbers p and q, $p \boxtimes q = p + (p + 1) + pq$.

For example, $2 \boxtimes 3 = 2 + (2 + 1) + 2 \times 3 = 11$.

17. What is the value of $4 \boxtimes 6$?

    (A) 24
    (B) 33
    (C) 34
    (D) 35
    (E) 40

18. If $M \boxtimes N = 4$, which of the following statements MUST be false?

    (A) M is a whole number.
    (B) N is equal to zero.
    (C) M is equal to zero.
    (D) M is an odd number.
    (E) M is equal to N.

---

19. 30% of $\frac{1}{4}x$ is equal to $\frac{1}{3}$ of 27. What is the value of x?

    (A) 3
    (B) 27
    (C) 80
    (D) 90
    (E) 120

---

20. What is the distance between Point A $(-5, 2)$ and Point B $(3, -4)$?

    (A) 6
    (B) 7
    (C) 8
    (D) 9
    (E) 10

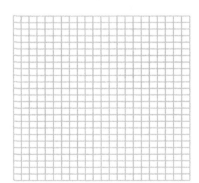

GO ON TO THE NEXT PAGE.

21. Hyung Seok is filming a documentary where people give short interviews. He has filmed a total of 8 hours of content, some on his handheld camera and some on his tripod camera. His tripod camera interviews are 5 minutes long, and his handheld camera interviews are 1 minute long. If Hyung Seok has interviewed a total of 160 people, how many tripod camera interviews has he completed?

   (A) 120
   (B) 80
   (C) 45
   (D) 30
   (E) 16

22. Kurt has g one-hundred dollar bills, h twenty dollar bills, and two dollars. Which of the following expressions represents his total amount of money, in dollars?

   (A) $g + h + 2$

   (B) $\dfrac{g}{100} + \dfrac{h}{20} + 2$

   (C) $20g + 100h + 2$

   (D) $100g + 20h + 2$

   (E) It cannot be determined from the information given.

23. In the figure to the right, a semicircle with an area of 12 intersects a triangle. If $x = 90$, what is the area of the shaded region?

   (A) 4
   (B) 6
   (C) 8
   (D) 9
   (E) 12

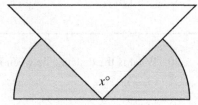

Note: figure not drawn to scale

GO ON TO THE NEXT PAGE.

24. If the minor arc in the figure to the right has an interior

angle of $\frac{5}{8}\pi$ radians, what is the length of the major

arc?

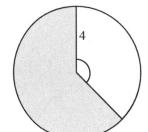

(A) $\frac{5}{8}\pi$

(B) $\frac{8}{5}\pi$

(C) $\frac{11}{2}\pi$

(D) $\frac{11}{8}\pi$

(E) 11π

25. 5 athletes competed on a team in a relay race, where each athlete ran 1 lap around a track. Catherine and William averaged 87 seconds per lap. Elizabeth, Rufus, and Henry averaged 97 seconds per lap. When all 5 laps were complete, what was the team's total time?

(A) 455 seconds

(B) 460 seconds

(C) 465 seconds

(D) 470 seconds

(E) 475 seconds

STOP

IF YOU FINISH BEFORE TIME IS CALLED,
YOU MAY CHECK YOUR WORK ON THIS SECTION ONLY.
DO NOT TURN TO ANY OTHER SECTION IN THE TEST.

Practice Test 2

How to Take this Practice Test

To simulate an accurate testing environment, sit at a desk in a quiet location free of distractions—no TV, computers, phones, music, or noise—and clear your desk of all materials except pencils and erasers. Remember that no calculators, rulers, protractors, dictionaries, or other aids are allowed on the SSAT.

Give yourself the following amounts of time for each section:

Section	Subject	Time Limit
	Writing	25 minutes
	5-minute break	
1	Math I	30 minutes
2	Reading	40 minutes
	5-minute break	
3	Verbal	30 minutes
4	Math II	30 minutes

Have an adult help you monitor your time, or use a stopwatch and time yourself. Only give yourself the allotted time for each section; put your pencil down when your time is up. Note: timing may be extended for students with diagnosed learning disabilities who apply for testing with accommodations.

Follow the instructions carefully. As you take your test, bubble your answers into the answer sheets provided. Use the test booklet as scratch paper for notes and calculations. Remember that you are not granted time at the end of a section to transfer your answers to the answer sheet, so you must do this as you go along.

When you are finished, check your answers against the answer keys provided. Then, score your exam using the directions at the end.

Be sure each mark completely fills the answer space.

Start with number 1 for each new section of the test. You may find more answer spaces than you need. If so, please leave them blank.

SECTION 1

1. Ⓐ Ⓑ Ⓒ Ⓓ Ⓔ	6. Ⓐ Ⓑ Ⓒ Ⓓ Ⓔ	11. Ⓐ Ⓑ Ⓒ Ⓓ Ⓔ	16. Ⓐ Ⓑ Ⓒ Ⓓ Ⓔ	21. Ⓐ Ⓑ Ⓒ Ⓓ Ⓔ
2. Ⓐ Ⓑ Ⓒ Ⓓ Ⓔ	7. Ⓐ Ⓑ Ⓒ Ⓓ Ⓔ	12. Ⓐ Ⓑ Ⓒ Ⓓ Ⓔ	17. Ⓐ Ⓑ Ⓒ Ⓓ Ⓔ	22. Ⓐ Ⓑ Ⓒ Ⓓ Ⓔ
3. Ⓐ Ⓑ Ⓒ Ⓓ Ⓔ	8. Ⓐ Ⓑ Ⓒ Ⓓ Ⓔ	13. Ⓐ Ⓑ Ⓒ Ⓓ Ⓔ	18. Ⓐ Ⓑ Ⓒ Ⓓ Ⓔ	23. Ⓐ Ⓑ Ⓒ Ⓓ Ⓔ
4. Ⓐ Ⓑ Ⓒ Ⓓ Ⓔ	9. Ⓐ Ⓑ Ⓒ Ⓓ Ⓔ	14. Ⓐ Ⓑ Ⓒ Ⓓ Ⓔ	19. Ⓐ Ⓑ Ⓒ Ⓓ Ⓔ	24. Ⓐ Ⓑ Ⓒ Ⓓ Ⓔ
5. Ⓐ Ⓑ Ⓒ Ⓓ Ⓔ	10. Ⓐ Ⓑ Ⓒ Ⓓ Ⓔ	15. Ⓐ Ⓑ Ⓒ Ⓓ Ⓔ	20. Ⓐ Ⓑ Ⓒ Ⓓ Ⓔ	25. Ⓐ Ⓑ Ⓒ Ⓓ Ⓔ

SECTION 2

1. Ⓐ Ⓑ Ⓒ Ⓓ Ⓔ	9. Ⓐ Ⓑ Ⓒ Ⓓ Ⓔ	17. Ⓐ Ⓑ Ⓒ Ⓓ Ⓔ	25. Ⓐ Ⓑ Ⓒ Ⓓ Ⓔ	33. Ⓐ Ⓑ Ⓒ Ⓓ Ⓔ
2. Ⓐ Ⓑ Ⓒ Ⓓ Ⓔ	10. Ⓐ Ⓑ Ⓒ Ⓓ Ⓔ	18. Ⓐ Ⓑ Ⓒ Ⓓ Ⓔ	26. Ⓐ Ⓑ Ⓒ Ⓓ Ⓔ	34. Ⓐ Ⓑ Ⓒ Ⓓ Ⓔ
3. Ⓐ Ⓑ Ⓒ Ⓓ Ⓔ	11. Ⓐ Ⓑ Ⓒ Ⓓ Ⓔ	19. Ⓐ Ⓑ Ⓒ Ⓓ Ⓔ	27. Ⓐ Ⓑ Ⓒ Ⓓ Ⓔ	35. Ⓐ Ⓑ Ⓒ Ⓓ Ⓔ
4. Ⓐ Ⓑ Ⓒ Ⓓ Ⓔ	12. Ⓐ Ⓑ Ⓒ Ⓓ Ⓔ	20. Ⓐ Ⓑ Ⓒ Ⓓ Ⓔ	28. Ⓐ Ⓑ Ⓒ Ⓓ Ⓔ	36. Ⓐ Ⓑ Ⓒ Ⓓ Ⓔ
5. Ⓐ Ⓑ Ⓒ Ⓓ Ⓔ	13. Ⓐ Ⓑ Ⓒ Ⓓ Ⓔ	21. Ⓐ Ⓑ Ⓒ Ⓓ Ⓔ	29. Ⓐ Ⓑ Ⓒ Ⓓ Ⓔ	37. Ⓐ Ⓑ Ⓒ Ⓓ Ⓔ
6. Ⓐ Ⓑ Ⓒ Ⓓ Ⓔ	14. Ⓐ Ⓑ Ⓒ Ⓓ Ⓔ	22. Ⓐ Ⓑ Ⓒ Ⓓ Ⓔ	30. Ⓐ Ⓑ Ⓒ Ⓓ Ⓔ	38. Ⓐ Ⓑ Ⓒ Ⓓ Ⓔ
7. Ⓐ Ⓑ Ⓒ Ⓓ Ⓔ	15. Ⓐ Ⓑ Ⓒ Ⓓ Ⓔ	23. Ⓐ Ⓑ Ⓒ Ⓓ Ⓔ	31. Ⓐ Ⓑ Ⓒ Ⓓ Ⓔ	39. Ⓐ Ⓑ Ⓒ Ⓓ Ⓔ
8. Ⓐ Ⓑ Ⓒ Ⓓ Ⓔ	16. Ⓐ Ⓑ Ⓒ Ⓓ Ⓔ	24. Ⓐ Ⓑ Ⓒ Ⓓ Ⓔ	32. Ⓐ Ⓑ Ⓒ Ⓓ Ⓔ	40. Ⓐ Ⓑ Ⓒ Ⓓ Ⓔ

SECTION 3

1. Ⓐ Ⓑ Ⓒ Ⓓ Ⓔ	13. Ⓐ Ⓑ Ⓒ Ⓓ Ⓔ	25. Ⓐ Ⓑ Ⓒ Ⓓ Ⓔ	37. Ⓐ Ⓑ Ⓒ Ⓓ Ⓔ	49. Ⓐ Ⓑ Ⓒ Ⓓ Ⓔ
2. Ⓐ Ⓑ Ⓒ Ⓓ Ⓔ	14. Ⓐ Ⓑ Ⓒ Ⓓ Ⓔ	26. Ⓐ Ⓑ Ⓒ Ⓓ Ⓔ	38. Ⓐ Ⓑ Ⓒ Ⓓ Ⓔ	50. Ⓐ Ⓑ Ⓒ Ⓓ Ⓔ
3. Ⓐ Ⓑ Ⓒ Ⓓ Ⓔ	15. Ⓐ Ⓑ Ⓒ Ⓓ Ⓔ	27. Ⓐ Ⓑ Ⓒ Ⓓ Ⓔ	39. Ⓐ Ⓑ Ⓒ Ⓓ Ⓔ	51. Ⓐ Ⓑ Ⓒ Ⓓ Ⓔ
4. Ⓐ Ⓑ Ⓒ Ⓓ Ⓔ	16. Ⓐ Ⓑ Ⓒ Ⓓ Ⓔ	28. Ⓐ Ⓑ Ⓒ Ⓓ Ⓔ	40. Ⓐ Ⓑ Ⓒ Ⓓ Ⓔ	52. Ⓐ Ⓑ Ⓒ Ⓓ Ⓔ
5. Ⓐ Ⓑ Ⓒ Ⓓ Ⓔ	17. Ⓐ Ⓑ Ⓒ Ⓓ Ⓔ	29. Ⓐ Ⓑ Ⓒ Ⓓ Ⓔ	41. Ⓐ Ⓑ Ⓒ Ⓓ Ⓔ	53. Ⓐ Ⓑ Ⓒ Ⓓ Ⓔ
6. Ⓐ Ⓑ Ⓒ Ⓓ Ⓔ	18. Ⓐ Ⓑ Ⓒ Ⓓ Ⓔ	30. Ⓐ Ⓑ Ⓒ Ⓓ Ⓔ	42. Ⓐ Ⓑ Ⓒ Ⓓ Ⓔ	54. Ⓐ Ⓑ Ⓒ Ⓓ Ⓔ
7. Ⓐ Ⓑ Ⓒ Ⓓ Ⓔ	19. Ⓐ Ⓑ Ⓒ Ⓓ Ⓔ	31. Ⓐ Ⓑ Ⓒ Ⓓ Ⓔ	43. Ⓐ Ⓑ Ⓒ Ⓓ Ⓔ	55. Ⓐ Ⓑ Ⓒ Ⓓ Ⓔ
8. Ⓐ Ⓑ Ⓒ Ⓓ Ⓔ	20. Ⓐ Ⓑ Ⓒ Ⓓ Ⓔ	32. Ⓐ Ⓑ Ⓒ Ⓓ Ⓔ	44. Ⓐ Ⓑ Ⓒ Ⓓ Ⓔ	56. Ⓐ Ⓑ Ⓒ Ⓓ Ⓔ
9. Ⓐ Ⓑ Ⓒ Ⓓ Ⓔ	21. Ⓐ Ⓑ Ⓒ Ⓓ Ⓔ	33. Ⓐ Ⓑ Ⓒ Ⓓ Ⓔ	45. Ⓐ Ⓑ Ⓒ Ⓓ Ⓔ	57. Ⓐ Ⓑ Ⓒ Ⓓ Ⓔ
10. Ⓐ Ⓑ Ⓒ Ⓓ Ⓔ	22. Ⓐ Ⓑ Ⓒ Ⓓ Ⓔ	34. Ⓐ Ⓑ Ⓒ Ⓓ Ⓔ	46. Ⓐ Ⓑ Ⓒ Ⓓ Ⓔ	58. Ⓐ Ⓑ Ⓒ Ⓓ Ⓔ
11. Ⓐ Ⓑ Ⓒ Ⓓ Ⓔ	23. Ⓐ Ⓑ Ⓒ Ⓓ Ⓔ	35. Ⓐ Ⓑ Ⓒ Ⓓ Ⓔ	47. Ⓐ Ⓑ Ⓒ Ⓓ Ⓔ	59. Ⓐ Ⓑ Ⓒ Ⓓ Ⓔ
12. Ⓐ Ⓑ Ⓒ Ⓓ Ⓔ	24. Ⓐ Ⓑ Ⓒ Ⓓ Ⓔ	36. Ⓐ Ⓑ Ⓒ Ⓓ Ⓔ	48. Ⓐ Ⓑ Ⓒ Ⓓ Ⓔ	60. Ⓐ Ⓑ Ⓒ Ⓓ Ⓔ

SECTION 4

1. Ⓐ Ⓑ Ⓒ Ⓓ Ⓔ	6. Ⓐ Ⓑ Ⓒ Ⓓ Ⓔ	11. Ⓐ Ⓑ Ⓒ Ⓓ Ⓔ	16. Ⓐ Ⓑ Ⓒ Ⓓ Ⓔ	21. Ⓐ Ⓑ Ⓒ Ⓓ Ⓔ
2. Ⓐ Ⓑ Ⓒ Ⓓ Ⓔ	7. Ⓐ Ⓑ Ⓒ Ⓓ Ⓔ	12. Ⓐ Ⓑ Ⓒ Ⓓ Ⓔ	17. Ⓐ Ⓑ Ⓒ Ⓓ Ⓔ	22. Ⓐ Ⓑ Ⓒ Ⓓ Ⓔ
3. Ⓐ Ⓑ Ⓒ Ⓓ Ⓔ	8. Ⓐ Ⓑ Ⓒ Ⓓ Ⓔ	13. Ⓐ Ⓑ Ⓒ Ⓓ Ⓔ	18. Ⓐ Ⓑ Ⓒ Ⓓ Ⓔ	23. Ⓐ Ⓑ Ⓒ Ⓓ Ⓔ
4. Ⓐ Ⓑ Ⓒ Ⓓ Ⓔ	9. Ⓐ Ⓑ Ⓒ Ⓓ Ⓔ	14. Ⓐ Ⓑ Ⓒ Ⓓ Ⓔ	19. Ⓐ Ⓑ Ⓒ Ⓓ Ⓔ	24. Ⓐ Ⓑ Ⓒ Ⓓ Ⓔ
5. Ⓐ Ⓑ Ⓒ Ⓓ Ⓔ	10. Ⓐ Ⓑ Ⓒ Ⓓ Ⓔ	15. Ⓐ Ⓑ Ⓒ Ⓓ Ⓔ	20. Ⓐ Ⓑ Ⓒ Ⓓ Ⓔ	25. Ⓐ Ⓑ Ⓒ Ⓓ Ⓔ

Writing Sample

Schools would like to get to know you better through a story you tell using one of the ideas below. Please choose the idea you find most interesting and write a story using the idea as your first sentence. Please fill in the circle next to the one you choose.

Ⓐ   What do you consider the three most important qualities of a good parent?

Ⓑ   They had never seen anything like it.

Use this page and the next page to complete your writing sample.

Continue on next page

Following each problem in this section, there are five suggested answers. Work out each problem in your head or in the blank space provided at the right of the page. Then look at the five suggested answers and decide which one is best.

Note: Figures that accompany problems in this section are drawn as accurately as possible EXCEPT when it is stated in a specific problem that its figure is not drawn to scale.

Sample problem:

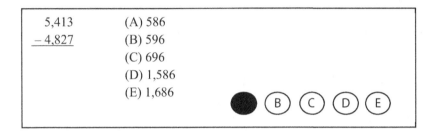

USE THIS SPACE FOR FIGURING.

1. There are 7 members in Peter's club. Peter currently has 10 cookies. If Peter wants to give 2 cookies to each member of his club, how many more cookies does he need to buy?

    (A) 2

    (B) 4

    (C) 6

    (D) 8

    (E) 9

---

2. Of the following, 3,567 divided by 41 is closest to

    (A) 10

    (B) 80

    (C) 90

    (D) 180

    (E) 900

GO ON TO THE NEXT PAGE.

3. Ashley has 21 pencils and Troy has 3. How many pencils must Ashley give Troy if each is to have the same number?

(A) 9

(B) 18

(C) 21

(D) 24

(E) It cannot be determined from the information given.

4. Mike has $x - 1$ notebooks. Jeff has two times the number of notebooks that Mike has. In terms of x, how many notebooks does Jeff have?

(A) $2x - 1$

(B) $x - 2$

(C) $x - 3$

(D) $2x - 2$

(E) $2x - 4$

5. $0.30 \times 1.8 =$

(A) 0.054

(B) 0.54

(C) 1.08

(D) 5.4

(E) 54

6. $1\frac{1}{4} + 2\frac{1}{8} + 3\frac{1}{16} =$

(A) $6\frac{1}{16}$

(B) $6\frac{7}{16}$

(C) $7\frac{1}{4}$

(D) $7\frac{6}{16}$

(E) $13\frac{1}{16}$

GO ON TO THE NEXT PAGE.

7. If $\frac{1}{4} + x > 1$, then x could be

    (A) $1/8$

    (B) $8/16$

    (C) $3/4$

    (D) $6/8$

    (E) $3/3$

8. Donna is 5 ft. 7 in. tall. Rachel is 3 in. shorter than Donna.
    If Elaina is 8 in. taller than Rachel, how tall is Elaina?

    (A) 5 ft. 6in.
    (B) 5 ft. 8 in.
    (C) 5 ft. 11 in.
    (D) 5 ft. 13 in.
    (E) 6 ft. 0 in.

9. If $3/_{6x} = 21$, then $1/_{3x} =$

    (A) 14
    (B) 18
    (C) 21
    (D) 36
    (E) 42

10. If 36 percent of b is 58, what is 18 percent of $2b$?

    (A) 29
    (B) 58
    (C) 116
    (D) 161
    (E) 322

GO ON TO THE NEXT PAGE.

11. A studio is covering a 4 meter by 8 meter wall with wallpaper. If the total cost of the wallpaper used is $104, how much does the wallpaper cost per square meter?

(A) $3.15

(B) $3.17

(C) $3.20

(D) $3.23

(E) $3.25

12. If $z + 3$ is an odd number, z could be equal to

(A) 1

(B) 3

(C) 5

(D) 21

(E) 22

13. If the sum of 4 consecutive even numbers is 60, the largest of these numbers is

(A) 14

(B) 16

(C) 18

(D) 20

(E) 22

14. If $N < 4$, which of the following CANNOT be a possible value of $3 - 2N$?

(A) –6

(B) –3

(C) 0

(D) 3

(E) 6

GO ON TO THE NEXT PAGE.

15. Over the course of her life, Sophia wrote 36 novels. If she wrote 9 novels before she was 30 years old, what percentage of her novels did she write when she was 30 years or older?

    (A) 25%
    (B) 30%
    (C) 40%
    (D) 60%
    (E) 75%

16. In the figure to the right, a square with a side length of 17 is adjacent to a square with a side length of 26. If the line segment where the two squares intersect has a length of 10, what is the perimeter of the whole figure?

    (A) 152
    (B) 154
    (C) 162
    (D) 164
    (E) 172

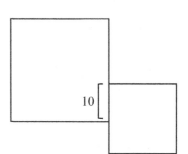

17. For what price is 30% off equal to $45 off?

    (A) $120
    (B) $130
    (C) $140
    (D) $150
    (E) $160

GO ON TO THE NEXT PAGE.

18. According to the graph to the right, which of the following statements is/are correct?

    I.   There are 5 more Fantasy books than Fiction books.

    II. There are more than twice as many Sci-Fi books as there are Horror books

    III. There are more Sci-Fi books than there are Fiction and Fantasy books combined.

    (A) I only

    (B) II only

    (C) I and II only

    (D) II and III only

    (E) I, II, and III

NUMBER OF BOOKS IN A LIBRARY

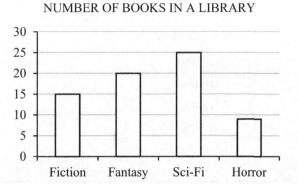

19. In the figure to the right, a square has a diagonal whose length is 14. What is the area of the square?

    (A) 25

    (B) 49

    (C) 50

    (D) 98

    (E) 00

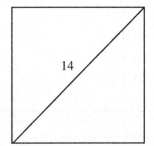

20. Joe's investment this year is worth $15,000, a 20% increase from last year's investment. What was Joe's investment worth last year?

    (A) $12,500

    (B) $12,750

    (C) $13,000

    (D) $14,980

    (E) $17,500

GO ON TO THE NEXT PAGE.

21. The function k is defined by $k(x) = (x)^2 + 2$. What is the value of $k(5)$?

    (A) 27
    (B) 25
    (C) 20
    (D) 14
    (E) 8

22. In a school of 100 students, students are enrolled in Spanish, French, or both Spanish and French classes. 45 students only take Spanish, and 19 students take both Spanish and French. How many total students take French?

    (A) 9
    (B) 36
    (C) 55
    (D) 64
    (E) 81

23. A number is increased by 12% and then decreased by 24%. The result is approximately what percent of the original number?

    (A) 12%
    (B) 15%
    (C) 24%
    (D) 85%
    (E) 115%

24. In the figure to the right, sector C has an area 2 times larger than sector B, and sector B has an area 2 times larger than sector A. If the radius of the circle is 2, what is the area of sector C?

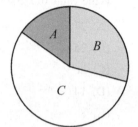

(A) $\frac{4}{7}\pi$

(B) $\frac{16}{7}\pi$

(C) $\frac{7}{16}\pi$

(D) $\frac{7}{4}\pi$

(E) $\frac{7}{2}\pi$

---

25. Which of the following is equivalent to $\sqrt{2} + \sqrt{9} + \sqrt{18}$?

(A) 31

(B) $6\sqrt{2}$

(C) $7\sqrt{2}$

(D) $2\sqrt{2} + 2\sqrt{9}$

(E) $3 + 4\sqrt{2}$

STOP

IF YOU FINISH BEFORE TIME IS CALLED,
YOU MAY CHECK YOUR WORK ON THIS SECTION ONLY.
DO NOT TURN TO ANY OTHER SECTION IN THE TEST.

Read each passage carefully and then answer the questions about it. For each question, decide on the basis of the passage which one of the choices best answers the question.

The Paleozoic ocean was dominated by animals known as nautiloids. These marine cephalopods were the main predators of the period, and were characterized by a tough external shell. In many species, the shell served not only as a form of protection, but also as a form of buoyancy control. The modern nautilus, for example—one of few surviving nautiloids—has a shell containing air-filled pockets, which

Line 5   help it to maintain neutral buoyancy in water.

Many modern cephalopods lack an external shell, but the shell usually isn't completely absent. Instead, modern cephalopods often possess an internal shell. In cuttlefish this shell is called the cuttlebone and, like the shell of the nautilus, contains gas filled pockets which help the cuttlefish to maintain buoyancy.

1. In this passage, the author's main purpose is to

(A) entertain

(B) speculate

(C) inform

(D) inquire

(E) debunk

2. Nautilus shells contain gas-filled pockets

(A) for the storage of food

(B) for buoyancy control

(C) to eliminate waste

(D) to capture prey

(E) for protection from predators

3. Based on the context of the passage, a "cephalopod" (line 6) most likely refers to

(A) any animal with a shell

(B) any marine predator

(C) a type of Nautilus

(D) an ancient nautiloid

(E) a type of animal that includes the Nautiloids

4. What would be the best title for this passage?

(A) The Shells of Nautiloids and Other Cephalopods

(B) How Nautiloids Swim

(C) The Difference Between a Cuttlefish and a Nautilus

(D) Predators of The Ancient Ocean

(E) Nautiloids: Living Fossils

GO ON TO THE NEXT PAGE.

5. It can be inferred from the passage that most nautiloids

    (A) possessed internal shells

    (B) hunted other nautiloids

    (C) are now extinct

    (D) could not swim

    (E) lacked external shells

GO ON TO THE NEXT PAGE.

A long time ago, when the world was much younger than it is now, people told and believed a great many wonderful stories about wonderful things which neither you nor I have ever seen. They often talked about a certain Mighty Being called Jupiter, or Zeus, who was king of the sky and the earth; and they said that he sat most of the time amid the clouds on the top of a very high mountain where he could

Line 5 look down and see everything that was going on in the earth beneath. He liked to ride on the storm-clouds and hurl burning thunderbolts right and left among the trees and rocks; and he was so very, very mighty that when he nodded, the earth quaked, the mountains trembled and smoked, the sky grew black, and the sun hid his face.

Jupiter had two brothers, both of them terrible fellows, but not nearly so great as himself. The

10 name of one of them was Neptune, or Poseidon, and he was the king of the sea. He had a glittering, golden palace far down in the deep sea-caves where the fishes live and the red coral grows; and whenever he was angry the waves would rise mountain high, and the storm-winds would howl fearfully, and the sea would try to break over the land; and men called him the Shaker of the Earth.

The other brother of Jupiter was a sad pale-faced being, whose kingdom was underneath the earth,

15 where the sun never shone and where there was darkness and weeping and sorrow all the time. His name was Pluto, or Aidoneus, and his country was called the Lower World, or the Land of Shadows, or Hades. Men said that whenever anyone died, Pluto would send his messenger, or Shadow Leader, to carry that one down into his cheerless kingdom; and for that reason they never spoke well of him, but thought of him only as the enemy of life.

6. What would be the best title for this passage?

(A) Weather Gods of the Ancient World
(B) How Gods are Made
(C) How the Planets Got Their Names
(D) The Origin of Hades
(E) Zeus and His Brothers

7. According to the passage, Neptune lived in

(A) undersea caverns
(B) the heavens
(C) a floating palace
(D) a storm cloud
(E) a mountain-high wave

8. The author's description of Pluto suggests that

(A) he was Jupiter's fiercest enemy
(B) he could control fire
(C) he could be harmed by sunlight
(D) he was evil and deceitful
(E) he was the king of the dead

GO ON TO THE NEXT PAGE.

9. Which of the following statements is implied by the passage?

(A) People once used myths to frighten children.

(B) People once controlled the weather by worshipping certain gods.

(C) People once used myths to help navigate the oceans.

(D) People once used myths as a way to explain natural events.

(E) People once used myths to impart morals and discourage criminal behavior.

GO ON TO THE NEXT PAGE.

In a settlement called Pormpuraaw, on the northern tip of the Cape York Peninsula in Queensland, Australia, live a people called the Thaayorre. The Thaayorre speak a language called Kuuk Thaayorre, which shares several important features with other aboriginal languages: it is spoken by only a few hundred people (two hundred and fifty, at the last count); most of the dialects have been lost as the number of speakers has dwindled; and, in Kuuk Thaayorre, there is no word for "left" or "right." In fact, in Kuuk Thaayorre there is no subjective direction at all. All sixteen words for direction relate to the cardinal directions: North, East, South and West.

Line 5

Kuuk Thaayorre uses cardinal directions instead of subjective direction at all scales, large and small. If you were speaking Kuuk Thaayorre, not only might you have to say something familiar like "you must walk north to reach the store," you might also have to say something like "your southeastern shoe is untied." If you lost track of your position relative to the cardinal directions, then you wouldn't be able to communicate effectively.

10

Owing to this peculiarity of their language, the Thaayorre people must always know which direction they are facing, even when they are inside or in unfamiliar surroundings. Fortunately, as recent research demonstrates, the Thaayorre and other people who speak similar languages have a special talent for that. They're even better at tracking their orientation than scientists had previously thought was possible.

15

Their abilities raise questions about the power of the human mind to achieve what was once thought impossible, and about the relationship between language and thought processes.

10. What does the author mean by "subjective direction" (line 6)?

(A) directions fixed to points in the world

(B) directions unique to aboriginal languages

(C) directions that rely on descriptions of landmarks

(D) directions that would be different from a different perspective

(E) directions that apply only to large objects

11. The author would most likely agree with which of the following statements about the Thaayorre people?

(A) They are very primitive.

(B) They cannot communicate effectively.

(C) They think more objectively than most other people.

(D) Their culture will soon be extinct.

(E) Their language and abilities raise questions about human potential.

GO ON TO THE NEXT PAGE.

12. The author implies that English speakers, unlike the Kuuk Thayyorre, normally use cardinal directions only

 (A) on large scales, for things that are big or far away

 (B) when they are inside

 (C) on small scales, for things that are small or nearby

 (D) when they cannot tell which way they are facing

 (E) when they are in familiar places

13. We can infer from the passage that

 (A) other aboriginal languages also rely on cardinal directions

 (B) scientists don't understand how we track subjective directions

 (C) cardinal directions are better than subjective directions

 (D) English has no words for cardinal directions

 (E) only the Thaayorre can speak Kuuk Thaayorre

GO ON TO THE NEXT PAGE.

Salt is often used as a de-icing agent on roads and sidewalks because a solution of salt and water has a lower freezing point than pure water. The ice exchanges molecules with the salt, creating a solution, and because this solution has a lower freezing point than pure water the ice usually melts. If the temperature is very cold, however, the ice may remain solid. In such cases, sand is spread over the surface of the ice in order to maintain traction, rather than trying to melt the ice.

Line 5

Salt is also added to ice to make cold brine. The chemical reaction that occurs as the salt melts the ice actually reduces the temperature of the solution, resulting in liquid water which is colder than the normal freezing point of water. This effect is used when making ice cream: a container of flavored cream is frozen by submerging it in cold brine while stirring, although care is taken to avoid letting the brine mix with the cream.

10

It is widely believed that salt also lowers the boiling point of water, but actually the opposite is true. Adding salt to water increases its boiling point, but it is a very small effect. Almost twelve teaspoons of salt would be required to increase the boiling point of an ounce of water by one degree Fahrenheit. However, while salt slightly increases the boiling point of water, it also causes it to heat more rapidly. Therefore, the addition of salt can cause water to boil faster than it would without salt.

15

14. People often spread salt on icy streets and sidewalks in order to

(A) generate heat that will melt the ice

(B) increase traction

(C) melt the ice by lowering its freezing point

(D) warn drivers of icy conditions

(E) make ice cream

15. Adding salt to water might cause it to boil sooner because

(A) salt lowers the boiling point

(B) the water will heat more quickly

(C) salt increases the boiling point

(D) adding salt to water generates heat

(E) salt melts ice

16. According to the passage, what is "brine" (line 6)?

(A) a solution of salt and water

(B) frozen saltwater

(C) boiling saltwater

(D) a solution of sand and ice

(E) an ingredient in ice cream

17. The author's style in this passage could best be described as

(A) argumentative

(B) expository

(C) narrative

(D) inquisitive

(E) condescending

GO ON TO THE NEXT PAGE.

18. What would be the best title for this passage?

    (A) How to Make Ice Cream

    (B) Boiling with Salt: Fact or Fiction?

    (C) Road Safety in Icy Conditions

    (D) The Many Uses of Salt

    (E) A Brief History of Salt

GO ON TO THE NEXT PAGE.

Then consider this startling situation: Arsene Lupin was wandering about within the limited bounds of a transatlantic steamer; in that very small corner of the world, in that dining saloon, in that smoking room, in that music room! Arsene Lupin was, perhaps, this gentleman... or that one... my neighbor at the table... the sharer of my stateroom...

Line 5   "And this condition of affairs will last for five days!" exclaimed Miss Nelly Underdown, next morning. "It is unbearable! I hope he will be arrested."

Then, addressing me, she added:

"And you, Monsieur d'Andrezy, you are on intimate terms with the captain; surely you know something?"

19. The passage implies that Arsene Lupin

(A) is a salesman

(B) knows the ship's captain

(C) has been arrested

(D) is a criminal

(E) is a friend of Monsieur d'Andrezy

20. Who is the narrator of this passage?

(A) Nelly Underdown

(B) Monsieur d'Andrezy

(C) Arsene Lupin

(D) the ship's captain

(E) an unnamed person

21. When the narrator describes the "limited bounds of a transatlantic steamer" (lines 1-2), he or she is suggesting that

(A) the steamer is a relatively small space

(B) the steamer travels slowly

(C) steamers are dangerous vehicles

(D) the steamer is very crowded

(E) the steamer's trip has a limited duration

22. The tone of the first paragraph creates a sense of

(A) suspense

(B) serenity

(C) hopelessness

(D) anger

(E) disgust

23. Based on the description in the passage, Nelly Underdown would be best described as

(A) forlorn

(B) secretive

(C) anxious

(D) depressed

(E) sea-sick

GO ON TO THE NEXT PAGE.

Chinese environmental officials are now raising the same concern that has worried environmental activists for years: that severe pollution has led to a rise of so-called "cancer villages." Activists and some journalists have been using the term "cancer villages" for several years to describe villages located close to waterways or industrial parks where cancer rates are very high.

Line 5   A report issued this week by China's Environment Ministry specifically mentions "cancer villages," blaming the problem on severe water and air pollution. It is thought to be one of the first times the term has been used by government officials. Official statistics indicate China has about 1,700 water pollution accidents each year and that up to 40 percent of the country's rivers are seriously polluted.

10   Water researcher Zhao Feihong at the Beijing Healthcare Association said last month that of the more than 100 rivers in Beijing only two or three can be used for tap water. "The rest of the rivers, if they have not dried up, then they are polluted by discharge," she said.

During the last week of January, smog hung over cities and towns from Liaoning in the north to as far south as Guangdong and air pollution reached unhealthy levels for long periods of time. Chinese *15*   officials blamed industrial activity, construction and the widespread use of coal for heat.

24. It can be inferred from the passage that heavy pollution

(A) occurs mainly around small villages

(B) causes an increase in cancer rates

(C) is only a problem in China

(D) increases the demand for heating coal

(E) mainly ends up in rivers

25. The passage was most likely taken from

(A) a novel

(B) a newspaper

(C) an encyclopedia

(D) a diary

(E) a letter

26. Which of the following is NOT cited as a possible cause for high rates of cancer in "cancer villages?"

(A) construction

(B) water pollution

(C) coal heating

(D) food contamination

(E) air pollution

27. What would the author most likely discuss next?

(A) other risk factors for cancer

(B) Chinese traditional medicine

(C) the various ministries in the Chinese government

(D) why some rivers can't be used for tap water

(E) possible solutions for the problem of "cancer villages"

GO ON TO THE NEXT PAGE.

In a survey of American Institutions, there seem to be three fundamental principles on which they are based: first, that all people are naturally equal in rights; second, that a people cannot be taxed without their own consent; and third, that they may delegate their power of self-government to representatives chosen by themselves.

Line 5
The remote origin of these principles it is difficult to trace. Some suppose that they are innate, appealing to consciousness—concerning which there can be no dispute or argument. Others suppose that they exist only so far as people can assert and use them, whether granted by rulers or seized by society. Some find that they arose among ancient Teutonic peoples in their German forests, while still others go back to Jewish, Grecian, and Roman history for their origin. Wherever they originated, their

10
practical enforcement has been a slow and unequal growth among various peoples, and it is always the evident result of a process of gradual change through time.

28. The author asserts that the values of American institutions

(A) are unique to the United States

(B) are guaranteed in all democracies

(C) are the same values as those of ancient Rome

(D) are the result of a long process of development

(E) are impossible to enforce

29. According to the passage, some people believe that the fundamental principles of American institutions first appear

(A) in the struggle against Britain

(B) at the Boston Tea Party

(C) in ancient Greek, Jewish, and Roman civilizations

(D) in the Constitution

(E) in the delegation of powers

30. Which motto best summarizes the second and third principles in lines 2-4?

(A) No Taxation Without Representation

(B) With Liberty and Justice for All

(C) From Many, One

(D) United We Stand, Divided We Fall

(E) Equality Before the Law

31. What does the author mean when he states that principles "exist only so far as people can assert and use them" (line 7)?

(A) Nobody actually has any principles.

(B) Rights only exist if they can be exercised

(C) You don't deserve something unless you can take it by force.

(D) People only have rights if they have a constitution.

(E) Animals do not have any rights.

32. The author's intention is to

(A) discuss the principles upon which American institutions are based

(B) persuade the reader of the correctness of American principles

(C) determine what makes American principles different from those of other nations

(D) criticize America's founding principles

(E) dispute false theories about American history

GO ON TO THE NEXT PAGE.

We stood together at the top of the cliff, in a dry and gentle breeze. A hawk hovered in the distance, riding the thermals. In that vast expanse, the only sound was the wind. We spoke in whispers, and she said "It's so quiet."

"I know" came my reply. Somehow those words didn't seem like enough, and I added "I bet if I *Line 5* shouted, it would echo for miles."

Turning to me, she asked "Why don't you?"

I thought about it. Why not? There's nothing hard about shouting. It seemed like it could be fun. But although I am ashamed to admit it, the keenest consideration was that it seemed as though I had been challenged. With my masculinity at stake I resolved to let out a manly shout and to make the *10* canyon echo with my voice; but as I took a breath, something restrained me.

There was a sacred quality in the vast depth of the silence, and it affected me. An aversion to blasphemy welled up inside me, and I could not compel myself to shatter the peace of the moment. I exhaled quietly, and as my breath mingled with the passing breeze I confessed "I don't think I can. It seems wrong."

15 "I know" she said, and we stood there a while longer without speaking. Eventually, we left the silence of the cliff and headed back to the trail; but the silence never left me—not entirely. In a peaceful moment, I can still hear it—and I still can't bring myself to break it.

33. Why did the narrator refrain from shouting?

(A) He suddenly felt short of breath.

(B) He didn't want to violate the sanctity of a peaceful moment.

(C) He was embarrassed to think that someone might hear him.

(D) He thought that it would be disgraceful to shout just because of a challenge.

(E) He was concerned that he might frighten the hawk.

34. Based on the context of the passage, "riding the thermals" (line 2) probably means that the hawk was

(A) flapping its wings

(B) hunting its prey

(C) diving from the sky

(D) calling to its mate

(E) gliding on the wind

35. What does the narrator mean when he says "the silence never left me" (line 16)?

(A) He was struck deaf.

(B) He is able to ignore loud noises by remembering the silence.

(C) He is still affected by the memory of the silence.

(D) He is now attracted to quiet places.

(E) The only thing he remembers about that day is the silence.

36. What best describes the narrator's attitude towards the silence of the cliff?

(A) reverent

(B) defiant

(C) resentful

(D) submissive

(E) confused

GO ON TO THE NEXT PAGE.

I met a traveller from an antique land
Who said: Two vast and trunkless legs of stone
Stand in the desert. Near them on the sand,
Half sunk, a shatter'd visage lies, whose frown

Line 5   And wrinkled lip and sneer of cold command
Tell that its sculptor well those passions read
Which yet survive, stamp'd on these lifeless things,
The hand that mock'd them and the heart that fed.
And on the pedestal these words appear:

10   "My name is Ozymandias, king of kings:
Look on my works, ye Mighty, and despair!"
Nothing beside remains: round the decay
Of that colossal wreck, boundless and bare,
The lone and level sands stretch far away.

37. What does the inscription in lines 10-11 suggest about Ozymandias?

(A) He knew that the statue would be the only thing left standing in that place.

(B) He hated other kings.

(C) He didn't want to build any more statues.

(D) He thought that his works exceeded all others.

(E) He was a kind and humble king.

38. What best describes the main message of this poem?

(A) Only love lasts forever.

(B) Stories can travel around the world.

(C) Even mighty empires succumb to time.

(D) Ozymandias was the greatest king.

(E) Sand eventually covers everything.

39. What best describes the tone of this poem?

(A) hateful

(B) disingenuous

(C) nostalgic

(D) humorous

(E) somber

40. The poem is written from the perspective of

(A) a traveler in a foreign land

(B) someone who is retelling a story

(C) Ozymandias, King of Kings

(D) a sculptor whose work is now ruined

(E) someone who has discovered an ancient statue

STOP

IF YOU FINISH BEFORE TIME IS CALLED,
YOU MAY CHECK YOUR WORK ON THIS SECTION ONLY.
DO NOT TURN TO ANY OTHER SECTION IN THE TEST.

This section consists of two different types of questions: synonyms and analogies. There are directions and a sample question for each type.

Synonyms

Each of the following questions consists of one word followed by five words or phrases. You are to select the one word or phrase whose meaning is closest to the word in capital letters.

Sample Question:

CHILLY:

(A) lazy
(B) nice
(C) dry
(D) cold
(E) sunny

Ⓐ Ⓑ Ⓒ ● Ⓔ

---

1. ILLICIT:

   (A) evil

   (B) untidy

   (C) prohibited

   (D) exaggerated

   (E) sultry

2. SOW:

   (A) stitch

   (B) pig

   (C) canal

   (D) till

   (E) irrigate

3. JEER:

   (A) praise

   (B) annoy

   (C) activate

   (D) mock

   (E) shake

4. KEEN:

   (A) sharp

   (B) indignant

   (C) wicked

   (D) above

   (E) askew

5. MIRTH:

   (A) gift

   (B) depression

   (C) clarity

   (D) gold

   (E) amusement

6. LINGER:

   (A) revert

   (B) delay

   (C) hurry

   (D) remark

   (E) ache

GO ON TO THE NEXT PAGE.

7. ADMIRE:

   (A) impugn
   (B) sing
   (C) count
   (D) adopt
   (E) respect

8. PERSECUTE:

   (A) assume
   (B) invade
   (C) govern
   (D) oppress
   (E) convict

9. APPREHENSIVE:

   (A) doubtful
   (B) captive
   (C) tidy
   (D) lost
   (E) just

10. COUNSEL:

   (A) letter
   (B) monitor
   (C) advice
   (D) carelessness
   (E) meeting

11. COMPOSURE:

   (A) self-control
   (B) author
   (C) preface
   (D) midpoint
   (E) conductor

12. IMMACULATE:

   (A) shackled
   (B) warranted
   (C) flawless
   (D) indigo
   (E) messy

13. TURBULENT:

   (A) breathless
   (B) drizzly
   (C) obnoxious
   (D) arrogant
   (E) disordered

14. LADEN:

   (A) burdened
   (B) upheld
   (C) submerged
   (D) broken
   (E) unjust

15. IMPEDE:

   (A) increase
   (B) ply
   (C) prepare
   (D) sail
   (E) block

16. EXPEDITE:

   (A) construct
   (B) incite
   (C) record
   (D) hurry
   (E) dabble

GO ON TO THE NEXT PAGE.

17. CONTAMINATE:

(A) destroy

(B) pollute

(C) exhaust

(D) merge

(E) consume

18. PARRY:

(A) deflect

(B) abridge

(C) collect

(D) exhale

(E) prohibit

19. NOTORIOUS:

(A) infamous

(B) masculine

(C) gelatinous

(D) numerous

(E) regular

20. EXUBERANT:

(A) magical

(B) slippery

(C) exhausted

(D) enthusiastic

(E) implied

21. ETERNAL:

(A) ephemeral

(B) internal

(C) final

(D) unending

(E) outside

22. BOLSTER:

(A) demolish

(B) support

(C) invite

(D) lock

(E) remake

23. EMACIATED:

(A) eviscerated

(B) ashen

(C) thin

(D) incarcerated

(E) wilted

24. NIMBLE:

(A) jumpy

(B) agile

(C) nervous

(D) soon

(E) runner

25. DIPLOMAT:

(A) governor

(B) representative

(C) ally

(D) nemesis

(E) general

26. PLUMMET:

(A) fall

(B) indicate

(C) celebrate

(D) hasten

(E) undermine

GO ON TO THE NEXT PAGE.

27. FRAUD:

   (A) deception

   (B) deterrent

   (C) propaganda

   (D) coercion

   (E) enforcer

28. MOLTEN:

   (A) shed

   (B) pursued

   (C) burnished

   (D) liquefied

   (E) glowing

29. SWINDLE:

   (A) open

   (B) invent

   (C) control

   (D) invert

   (E) cheat

30. INVISIBLE:

   (A) silent

   (B) unseen

   (C) buried

   (D) secure

   (E) unpredictable

GO ON TO THE NEXT PAGE.

Analogies

The following questions ask you to find relationships between words. For each question, select the answer choice that best completes the meaning of the sentence.

Sample Question:

Kitten is to cat as

(A) fawn is to colt
(B) puppy is to dog
(C) cow is to bull
(D) wolf is to bear
(E) hen is to rooster

Choice (B) is the best answer because a kitten is a young cat just as a puppy is a young dog. Of all the answer choices, (B) states a relationship that is most like the relationship between kitten and cat.

---

31. Grapes are to wine as

    (A) bread is to toast

    (B) tomato is to salad

    (C) milk is to cheese

    (D) happiness is to song

    (E) melons are to seeds

32. Tailor is to clothing as

    (A) nanny is to children

    (B) cobbler is to shoes

    (C) miller is to grain

    (D) banker is to business

    (E) officer is to army

33. Subtle is to obvious as

    (A) shadow is to pale

    (B) inferred is to implied

    (C) meek is to timid

    (D) bright is to sunny

    (E) quiet is to loud

34. Bat is to racket as

    (A) baseball is to tennis ball

    (B) game is to player

    (C) soccer is to kickball

    (D) basketball is to net

    (E) goalie is to hockey

35. Ambassador is to diplomacy as

    (A) president is to nation

    (B) clerk is to documents

    (C) spy is to espionage

    (D) covert is to hidden

    (E) initiate is to veteran

36. Actor is to theater as

    (A) audience is to speech

    (B) singer is to music

    (C) painter is to easel

    (D) hangar is to aircraft

    (E) lawyer is to courtroom

GO ON TO THE NEXT PAGE.

37. Sweet is to savory as

    (A) taste is to sour

    (B) color is to red

    (C) sugar is to salt

    (D) flavor is to odor

    (E) dessert is to enjoy

38. Refute is to argument as

    (A) debunk is to myth

    (B) quarrel is to sibling

    (C) concede is to debate

    (D) descend is to precipice

    (E) compete is to opponent

39. Water is to pipe as

    (A) ocean is to sea

    (B) liquid is to jug

    (C) electricity is to wire

    (D) driver is to car

    (E) cloud is to storm

40. Annoyed is to distraught as

    (A) visited is to deported

    (B) guilty is to convicted

    (C) moody is to depressed

    (D) amused is to pleased

    (E) arrested is to detained

41. Indigenous is to native as foreign is to

    (A) commerce

    (B) domestic

    (C) unusual

    (D) government

    (E) alien

42. Antiseptic is to germs as

    (A) fertilizer is to plants

    (B) bandage is to wounds

    (C) bleach is to clothes

    (D) pesticide is to insects

    (E) kindling is to fires

43. Guts are to bravery as

    (A) hearts are to circulation

    (B) feet are to leg

    (C) wrists are to writing

    (D) lungs are to confidence

    (E) brains are to intelligence

44. Botched is to ineptly as perfect is to

    (A) expertly

    (B) implicitly

    (C) poorly

    (D) quickly

    (E) hardly

45. Principal is to school as

    (A) surgeon is to operation

    (B) farmer is to plow

    (C) foreman is to factory

    (D) author is to novel

    (E) policeman is to arrest

46. Vow is to promise as epiphany is to

    (A) oath

    (B) speech

    (C) confusion

    (D) silence

    (E) realization

GO ON TO THE NEXT PAGE.

47. Habit is to individual as

(A) law is to judge

(B) tradition is to practice

(C) custom is to society

(D) culture is to global

(E) consensus is to group

48. Indifferent is to apathy as

(A) placid is to vigor

(B) provocation is to anger

(C) suspicious is to trust

(D) vexed is to anxiety

(E) annoyed is to nuisance

49. Papyrus is to scroll as

(A) vellum is to skin

(B) clay is to tablet

(C) percussion is to instrument

(D) chapter is to book

(E) feather is to bird

50. Cavernous is to hollow as calamitous is to

(A) important

(B) uneventful

(C) unfortunate

(D) typical

(E) deep

51. Douse is to flame as

(A) wreck is to car

(B) rain is to weather

(C) quash is to rebellion

(D) lamp is to light

(E) captivate is to audience

52. Jaywalker is to criminal as

(A) prisoner is to warden

(B) soil is to earth

(C) collision is to injury

(D) misdemeanor is to felony

(E) legal is to illegal

53. Sated is to ravenous as quenched is to

(A) parched

(B) thirst

(C) barren

(D) hungry

(E) appetite

54. Generous is to philanthropist as

(A) unlikely is to outcome

(B) stingy is to miser

(C) merciless is to victim

(D) wealthy is to accountant

(E) virtuous is to philosopher

55. Transgress is to law as

(A) commit is to crime

(B) decide is to selection

(C) ignore is to avoidance

(D) study is to prepare

(E) violate is to agreement

56. Jettison is to cargo as

(A) deliver is to parcel

(B) flotsam is to debris

(C) immigrate is to nation

(D) evict is to tenant

(E) passenger is to ship

GO ON TO THE NEXT PAGE.

57. Saunter is to sprint as drizzle is to

(A) hail

(B) speed

(C) pour

(D) taste

(E) trickle

58. Botanist is to plants as

(A) economist is to newspaper

(B) geologist is to minerals

(C) impressionist is to people

(D) astronomer is to astronauts

(E) meteorologist is to forecasts

59. Prohibit is to allow as

(A) entice is to lure

(B) assume is to fact

(C) personal is to individual

(D) encourage is to dissuade

(E) disown is to forget

60. Evaporate is to condense as

(A) thaw is to freeze

(B) heat is to liquid

(C) boil is to dry

(D) snow is to rain

(E) water is to steam

STOP

IF YOU FINISH BEFORE TIME IS CALLED,
YOU MAY CHECK YOUR WORK ON THIS SECTION ONLY.
DO NOT TURN TO ANY OTHER SECTION IN THE TEST.

SECTION 4
25 Questions

Following each problem in this section, there are five suggested answers. Work out each problem in your head or in the blank space provided at the right of the page. Then look at the five suggested answers and decide which one is best.

Note: Figures that accompany problems in this section are drawn as accurately as possible EXCEPT when it is stated in a specific problem that its figure is not drawn to scale.

Sample problem:

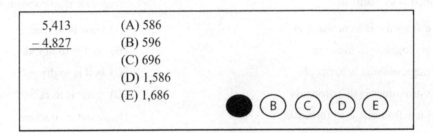

USE THIS SPACE FOR FIGURING.

1. In the figure to the right, the perimeter of the polygon is 60. If all the sides in the polygon are of equal length, what is the length of one side?

   (A) 12
   (B) 15
   (C) 16
   (D) 20
   (E) 60

---

2. 13 divides evenly into which of the following numbers?

   (A) 141
   (B) 142
   (C) 143
   (D) 144
   (E) 145

GO ON TO THE NEXT PAGE.

Practice Tests

3. $2\frac{4}{6} + 2\frac{2}{4} =$

    (A) $4\frac{4}{10}$

    (B) $4\frac{8}{10}$

    (C) $4\frac{6}{10}$

    (D) $5\frac{1}{6}$

    (E) $5\frac{10}{6}$

Questions 4-5 are based on the graph to the right.

4. How many fewer waffles were sold on Friday than on Sunday?

    (A) 2

    (B) 20

    (C) 25

    (D) 2000

    (E) 3000

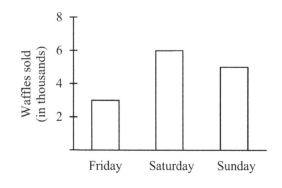

5. The number of waffles sold on Saturday is about how many times the number of waffles sold on Sunday?

    (A) 0.25

    (B) 0.75

    (C) 1.20

    (D) 1.80

    (E) 25

---

6. Which of the following is equivalent to the expression $x^2 - 3x - 54$?

    (A) $(x - 6)(x - 9)$

    (B) $(x - 6)(x + 9)$

    (C) $(x + 6)(x - 9)$

    (D) $(x + 3)(x - 18)$

    (E) $(x - 3)(x - 18)$

GO ON TO THE NEXT PAGE.

7. The remainder when 57 is divided by 6 is equivalent to the remainder when 65 is divided by

    (A) 5
    (B) 15
    (C) 30
    (D) 31
    (E) 63

8. If $\frac{3}{2}x > 6$, then x could be

    (A) 1
    (B) 2
    (C) 3
    (D) 4
    (E) 5

9. On the number line to the right, which letter represents the number 24?

    (A) A
    (B) B
    (C) C
    (D) D
    (E) None of the above.

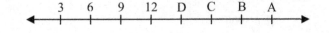

10. If 3 cartons weigh 16 pounds, what is the weight of 7.5 cartons?

    (A) 16 pounds
    (B) 32 pounds
    (C) 36 pounds
    (D) 40 pounds
    (E) 120 pounds

GO ON TO THE NEXT PAGE.

11. For any numbers p and s, $p \blacksquare s = p + 2s$.

For example, $4 \blacksquare 5 = 4 + 2 \times 5 = 14$.

Which expression best represents the value of $p \blacksquare 3$?

(A) $p + 3$

(B) $p + 6$

(C) $p + 3s$

(D) $p + 6s$

(E) $2p + 3$

12. Jane lives 4 miles away from school. If Sasha lives 3 miles away from school, what is the distance between Jane's home and Sasha's home, in miles?

(A) 1

(B) 2

(C) 4

(D) 7

(E) It cannot be determined from the information given.

13. In the figure to the right, what is the length of side x?

(A) 1.5

(B) 2

(C) 3

(D) 6

(E) 7

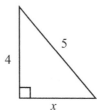

GO ON TO THE NEXT PAGE.

14. There are 6 officials waiting to ride in a limo. If there are 4 limos and at least one official must ride in each limo, what is the greatest number of officials who could ride in one limo?

(A) 2

(B) 3

(C) 4

(D) 5

(E) 6

15. In the figure to the right, what is the value of x?

(A) 10

(B) 20

(C) 30

(D) 40

(E) 50

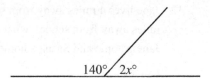

$140°$ $2x°$

16. A company has 3 full-time employees and 4 part-time employees. The full-time employees each work an average of 8 hours a day and the part-time employees each work an average of 4.5 hours a day. For all 7 employees, the average number of hours worked per day is

(A) 5.5

(B) 6

(C) 6.5

(D) 12.5

(E) It cannot be determined from the information given.

17. If $2A + D = 6$ and $D + A = 3$, what is the value of D?

(A) 0

(B) 1

(C) 2

(D) 3

(E) 6

GO ON TO THE NEXT PAGE.

18. A small cube has a side length of 3 inches. How many small cubes are needed to make a large cube with a side length of 12 inches?

    (A) 4

    (B) 16

    (C) 32

    (D) 64

    (E) 128

19. There are an equal number of motorcycles and cars in a garage. If the sum of the number of motorcycle wheels and car wheels equals 30, how many motorcycles are in the garage?

    (A) 3

    (B) 4

    (C) 5

    (D) 6

    (E) 15

20. Harvey's total commute is 1 hour and 30 minutes long. How long does it take Harvey to complete two-thirds of his commute?

    (A) 20 minutes

    (B) 30 minutes

    (C) 45 minutes

    (D) 50 minutes

    (E) 60 minutes

21. 20% of a is equal to b. What is 35% of b, in terms of a?

    (A) $0.07a$

    (B) $0.14a$

    (C) $0.15a$

    (D) $0.35a$

    (E) $0.70a$

GO ON TO THE NEXT PAGE.

22. If $a = \frac{2}{3}b$ and $c = \frac{1}{2}b$, c is equal to

(A) $a/4$

(B) $\frac{3a}{4}$

(C) a

(D) ab

(E) $\frac{4a}{3}$

---

23. $4\overline{)733}$

(A) $\frac{730}{4} + 3$

(B) $\frac{700}{4} + 33$

(C) $\frac{700 \times 30 \times 2}{4}$

(D) $\frac{7}{4} + \frac{3}{4} + \frac{3}{4}$

(E) $\frac{700}{4} + \frac{30}{4} + \frac{3}{4}$

---

24. $$(x + 6)(2x - 4)$$

Which of the following is equivalent to the expression above?

(A) $2x^2 - 12x + 24$

(B) $2x^2 + 8x - 18$

(C) $2x^2 - 12x - 24$

(D) $2x^2 + 8x - 24$

(E) $2x^2 + 16x - 12$

GO ON TO THE NEXT PAGE.

25. The slope of a line that is parallel to $-3x + 2y = 5$ is

(A) $-3/2$

(B) $-2/3$

(C) $2/5$

(D) $2/3$

(E) $3/2$

STOP

IF YOU FINISH BEFORE TIME IS CALLED,
YOU MAY CHECK YOUR WORK ON THIS SECTION ONLY.
DO NOT TURN TO ANY OTHER SECTION IN THE TEST.

Answers and Scoring
Chapter 4

Practice Test 1

Section 1 (Pages 37-44)

1. A	6. C	11. C	16. E	21. E
2. D	7. C	12. B	17. B	22. C
3. D	8. A	13. B	18. D	23. E
4. B	9. C	14. E	19. E	24. A
5. B	10. D	15. A	20. E	25. B

Section 2 (Pages 46-60)

1. D	9. E	17. C	25. A	33. B
2. B	10. D	18. B	26. B	34. D
3. B	11. D	19. C	27. D	35. E
4. E	12. E	20. B	28. B	36. D
5. C	13. B	21. B	29. A	37. A
6. C	14. D	22. D	30. D	38. B
7. A	15. B	23. E	31. C	39. E
8. B	16. C	24. C	32. A	40. D

Section 3 (Pages 62-69)

1. C	13. D	25. C	37. B	49. A
2. E	14. E	26. A	38. C	50. D
3. B	15. D	27. A	39. A	51. A
4. B	16. C	28. C	40. B	52. C
5. E	17. C	29. E	41. E	53. E
6. B	18. A	30. D	42. B	54. D
7. A	19. D	31. C	43. B	55. B
8. C	20. A	32. B	44. E	56. C
9. D	21. D	33. E	45. B	57. E
10. C	22. A	34. D	46. D	58. A
11. D	23. B	35. C	47. D	59. C
12. B	24. E	36. A	48. B	60. A

Section 4 (Pages 70-77)

1. B	6. E	11. A	16. A	21. B
2. D	7. D	12. A	17. B	22. D
3. B	8. A	13. D	18. C	23. B
4. E	9. B	14. C	19. E	24. C
5. C	10. D	15. B	20. E	25. C

Scoring Your Test

First, count up the number of questions you answered correctly, the number of questions you skipped, and the number of questions you answered incorrectly. Then, calculate your raw score using the following formula:

$$\text{Raw Score} = \text{\# of questions correct} - \frac{\text{\# of questions incorrect}}{4}$$

Add together your raw scores from your two math sections in order to determine your total raw math score.

Once you have found your raw score, convert it into an approximate scaled score using the estimated scoring charts on the next page. Keep in mind that you may score within 100 points of this estimate when you take your actual SSAT exam.

My Raw Score for Practice Test 1					
Section	# of Questions Correct		# of Questions Incorrect		Raw Score
Verbal		−	÷ 4	=	
Reading		−	÷ 4	=	
Math 1 + Math 2		−	÷ 4	=	

Scaled Score

Once you have found your raw score, convert it into an approximate **scaled score** using the scoring charts that follow. These charts provide an estimate for your SSAT scaled score based on your performance on this practice test. Keep in mind that your scaled score may differ within 100 points of this estimate when you take your actual SSAT exam, depending on the SSAT's specific scaling for that exam and any differences in your own test-taking process.

Upper Level Scaled Scores			
Raw Score	Math	Reading	Verbal
60			800
55			800
50	800		780
45	780		750
40	755	800	725
35	725	720	700
30	700	690	645
25	670	660	645
20	640	630	615
15	615	600	590
10	585	570	565
5	555	540	530
0	530	510	505
-5	500	500	500
-10 and lower	500	500	500

Percentile

When you take your actual SSAT exam, you will also receive a **percentile** ranking comparing your performance against the performance of other students of your gender and grade who have taken the SSAT within the past three years. For example, a percentile of 62 means that you scored higher than 62% of other SSAT test-takers of your gender and grade. Because your percentile ranking shows how well you performed according to your own grade level, these rankings are frequently given the most consideration by admissions offices.

The following chart provides an estimate of your SSAT percentile ranking based on your **raw scores** for this practice test. Keep in mind that the percentiles below are estimates only and are not specific to your own grade and gender. Because younger students are expected to score differently than older students on this exam, your percentile may be higher or lower than this estimate depending on your grade.

Upper Level Percentiles			
Raw Score	Math	Reading	Verbal
60			99
55			99
50	99		98
45	96		94
40	87	99	87
35	75	94	77
30	62	78	63
25	45	57	47
20	30	36	31
15	18	20	18
10	9	8	8
5	3	3	3
0	1	1	1
-5	1	1	1
-10 and lower	1	1	1

The following chart shows the median (50th percentile) **scaled scores** for each grade level. If you are scoring at the median for your grade level, this means that you scored higher than half of your peers.

Upper Level Median Scores			
Grade	Math	Reading	Verbal
Grade 8	676	647	660
Grade 9	699	653	667
Grade 10	705	659	670
Grade 11	704	647	656

Practice Test 2

Section 1 (Pages 87-94)

1. B	6. B	11. E	16. A	21. A
2. C	7. E	12. E	17. D	22. C
3. A	8. E	13. C	18. C	23. D
4. D	9. A	14. A	19. D	24. B
5. B	10. B	15. E	20. A	25. E

Section 2 (Pages 96-108)

1. C	9. D	17. B	25. B	33. B
2. B	10. D	18. D	26. D	34. E
3. E	11. E	19. D	27. E	35. C
4. A	12. A	20. B	28. D	36. A
5. C	13. A	21. A	29. C	37. D
6. E	14. C	22. A	30. A	38. C
7. A	15. B	23. C	31. B	39. E
8. E	16. A	24. B	32. A	40. B

Section 3 (Pages 110-117)

1. C	13. E	25. B	37. C	49. B
2. B	14. A	26. A	38. A	50. C
3. D	15. E	27. A	39. C	51. C
4. A	16. D	28. D	40. C	52. D
5. E	17. B	29. E	41. E	53. A
6. B	18. A	30. B	42. D	54. B
7. E	19. A	31. C	43. E	55. E
8. D	20. D	32. B	44. A	56. D
9. A	21. D	33. E	45. C	57. C
10. C	22. B	34. A	46. E	58. B
11. A	23. C	35. C	47. C	59. D
12. C	24. B	36. E	48. D	60. A

Section 4 (Pages 118-125)

1. A	6. C	11. B	16. B	21. A
2. C	7. D	12. E	17. A	22. B
3. D	8. E	13. C	18. D	23. E
4. D	9. A	14. B	19. C	24. D
5. C	10. D	15. B	20. E	25. E

Scoring Your Test

First, count up the number of questions you answered correctly, the number of questions you skipped, and the number of questions you answered incorrectly. Then, calculate your raw score using the following formula:

$$\text{Raw Score} = \text{\# of questions correct} - \frac{\text{\# of questions incorrect}}{4}$$

Add together your raw scores from your two math sections in order to determine your total raw math score.

Once you have found your raw score, convert it into an approximate scaled score using the estimated scoring charts on the next page. Keep in mind that you may score within 100 points of this estimate when you take your actual SSAT exam.

My Raw Score for Practice Test 2			
Section	# of Questions Correct	# of Questions Incorrect	Raw Score
Verbal	−	÷ 4 =	
Reading	−	÷ 4 =	
Math 1 + Math 2	−	÷ 4 =	

Scaled Score

Once you have found your raw score, convert it into an approximate **scaled score** using the scoring charts that follow. These charts provide an estimate for your SSAT scaled score based on your performance on this practice test. Keep in mind that your scaled score may differ within 100 points of this estimate when you take your actual SSAT exam, depending on the SSAT's specific scaling for that exam and any differences in your own test-taking process.

	Upper Level Scaled Scores		
Raw Score	Math	Reading	Verbal
60			800
55			800
50	800		780
45	780		750
40	755	800	725
35	725	720	700
30	700	690	645
25	670	660	645
20	640	630	615
15	615	600	590
10	585	570	565
5	555	540	530
0	530	510	505
-5	500	500	500
-10 and lower	500	500	500

Percentile

When you take your actual SSAT exam, you will also receive a **percentile** ranking comparing your performance against the performance of other students of your gender and grade who have taken the SSAT within the past three years. For example, a percentile of 62 means that you scored higher than 62% of other SSAT test-takers of your gender and grade. Because your percentile ranking shows how well you performed according to your own grade level, these rankings are frequently given the most consideration by admissions offices.

The following chart provides an estimate of your SSAT percentile ranking based on your **raw scores** for this practice test. Keep in mind that the percentiles below are estimates only and are not specific to your own grade and gender. Because younger students are expected to score differently than older students on this exam, your percentile may be higher or lower than this estimate depending on your grade.

Upper Level Percentiles			
Raw Score	Math	Reading	Verbal
60			99
55			99
50	99		98
45	96		94
40	87	99	87
35	75	94	77
30	62	78	63
25	45	57	47
20	30	36	31
15	18	20	18
10	9	8	8
5	3	3	3
0	1	1	1
-5	1	1	1
-10 and lower	1	1	1

The following chart shows the median (50th percentile) **scaled scores** for each grade level. If you are scoring at the median for your grade level, this means that you scored higher than half of your peers.

Upper Level Median Scores			
Grade	Math	Reading	Verbal
Grade 8	676	647	660
Grade 9	699	653	667
Grade 10	705	659	670
Grade 11	704	647	656